# INDIAN CONSTITUTIONAL REFORM

# INDIAN CONSTITUTIONAL REFORM

VIEWED IN THE LIGHT OF HISTORY

**VINCENT A. SMITH**

**C. I. E. ; M. A. ; HON. LITT. D. (DUBL.) ; I.C. S. RETD.**

GYAN

*Published by*

Gyan Publishing House
5, Ansari Road
Daryaganj, New Delhi-110002
Phone: 011-47034999, 9811692060
E-mail: books@gyanbooks.com

*Distribution Network*
gyanbooks.com
India, USA, Canada, UK, Australia, France



ISBN: 978-81-212-8776-0 (PB)
First Published, 1919

2nd Impression 2023

*Printed at:* Gyan Press, Delhi.



**INDIAN CONSTITUTIONAL REFORM**
Author: Vincent A. Smith

# INDIAN CONSTITUTIONAL REFORM

## *VIEWED IN THE LIGHT OF HISTORY*

BY

VINCENT A. SMITH

C.I.E.; M.A.; Hon. Litt.D. (Dubl.); I.C.S. Retd.

AUTHOR OF 'THE EARLY HISTORY OF INDIA', 'THE OXFORD HISTORY OF INDIA', ETC.

HUMPHREY MILFORD

OXFORD UNIVERSITY PRESS

LONDON EDINBURGH GLASGOW NEW YORK

TORONTO MELBOURNE CAPE TOWN BOMBAY

1919

# PREFACE

The authors of the *Report on Indian Constitutional Reforms* (1918) insist that 'full and public discussion is necessary', and ask that their proposals may be allowed to 'benefit by reasoned criticism both in England and India, official and non-official alike'. That comprehensive invitation dispenses with the necessity of apology for intervention in the discussion by any person equipped to a reasonable degree with qualifications entitling him to form and express an opinion on the subject. My official experience during twenty-nine years in revenue, 'settlement', executive, judicial, and administrative duties gives me some title to deal with the question of reform from the point of view of an officer who has had in his time practical knowledge of the working of the government machine. The study of Indian history in all its branches for almost half a century entitles me to speak with some authority concerning the historical background which lies behind the stage on which the drama of present-day politics is played. It is simply impossible to understand modern India even tolerably well without a moderate acquaintance with the past in which the roots of the present are so deeply buried. The authors of the Report, in their haste to give India the benefit of up-to-date democratic formulae, have shown little regard to the lessons of history. The defects of the Report in that respect, which have been noticed by several critics, forced themselves upon my attention, and I could not help feeling that my special knowledge might possibly be of service if placed at the disposal of readers interested in the reform problem, while unskilled in that unpopular subject, Indian History. My inclination would lead me to continue my life-long studies and to avoid the muddy waters of current politics. But India has done much for me, and now, before my working days come to an end, I should like to do something for India, by contributing my mite towards the solution of the dangerous problem which Parliament must solve one way or another without long delay. It is unnecessary to dilate upon the dangers of the experiments advocated by the Secretary of State, the Viceroy, and many reformers of less note. The rather lurid language of the Report about the 'disaster' and 'misery' which will follow on the failure of their plans is even stronger than any words I should care to use. It is evident that their confidence lacks robustness. Perhaps Mr. J. A. R. Marriott, M.P., may not be altogether wrong when he calls the scheme of the Report 'a Gargantuan gamble'. If there be any truth in that view, which is not inconsistent with the rhetoric of the authors, it is permissible to remark that the Indian Empire is a large stake to play with.

It is wrong to suppose that the Report 'holds the field', and that the issue is 'the Report or nothing'. That view is wholly erroneous, as will be apparent to anybody who has read, as I have done, the numerous books by H.H. the Aga Khan, Mr. Vyasa Rao, and other authors, not to speak of the multitude of speeches, articles, and pamphlets pouring continually from the press.[1] The Report omits much that needs consideration and includes much that could be spared.

[1] A very useful work for reference is *Indian Constitutional Documents (1600-1918)*, by Panchanandan Das Mukherji, 2nd ed., vol. i, 803 pages, vol. ii, 100 pages: Thacker, Spink & Co., Calcutta, 1918; price 13 rupees.

Recent events, and above all the Great War, fraught as it is with incalculable consequences, render a change in the method of governing India imperative. That cardinal fact is acknowledged by me quite as heartily and sincerely as it is by Mr. Montagu and Lord Chelmsford. But I do not feel bound to admire the whole of their work or to accept their principles without demur. These principles, on the contrary, demand the most searching scrutiny and, in my personal opinion, are largely erroneous. I agree that 'self-government' and the increased employment of Indians in the public service, as stated in the 'Pronouncement', are objects not only desirable, but attainable within certain limits. The emphasis laid upon those limits in this essay is imposed by the historical method of treatment and should not be misunderstood. It does not imply hostility to reasonable, practical reforms. I say frankly that I think it is a mistake to seek the distant 'goal of responsible government' at present. The premature chase after 'responsible government' is the cause of nearly all the illogical and contradictory recommendations of the Report, as its authors confess in paragraph 354. If they had postponed the consideration of 'responsible government' to a more convenient season they would have done much better. They have run to some extent ahead of the 'Pronouncement' which they profess to follow. 'Responsible government' in the English parliamentary sense may or may not be a suitable 'goal' for Indian politicians, but, however that may be, it is better left alone just now. Even without it the reformers have plenty to do.

Chapters 3 and 4 of this essay treat faithfully and candidly of certain disagreeable, inconvenient facts, which are shirked or slurred over by the authors of the Report. It is no use to pretend blindness to awkward realities which are not affected by the pretending. Only the truth can make us free. . The excessive optimism of the Secretary of State and the Viceroy, as illustrated by the quotations in Chapter 5, is not justified by the realities of the situation.

In the concluding chapter I have attempted to indicate methods by which genuine, useful reforms seem to be attainable.

My whole adult life for fifty years has been dedicated to India, and the sole purpose of this little book is to offer some help, however small, to the persons, especially the members of both Houses of Parliament, who are responsible for the final decision which concerns India so deeply, and England also. I do not very much care whether particular suggestions are accepted or not. The essential thing is that the whole of the facts, agreeable or disagreeable, convenient or inconvenient, should be faced squarely, and that the decision should be based upon truth, not upon illusion. The 'Māyā', which 'sends forth an imaged world, just as a magician produces illusive effects', permeates the Report.

V. A. S.

OXFORD, *Dec.* 18, 1918.

I.

'That sound public opinion, which it is so essential to carry along with every branch of our free government, has been very partially exercised with regard to Indian affairs. The problem of the best mode of governing that country is so difficult to be solved, the interests affected by it so remote and complicated, that few have given it any deep attention' (Sir John Malcolm, *The Political History of India*, 1826, vol. ii, p. 114).

II.

'Hitherto they [*scil.* "the voiceless millions of India"] have regarded the official as their representative in the councils of government; and now we have to tear up their faith by the roots, to teach them that in future they must bring their troubles to the notice of an elected representative—further, that they have the power to compel his attention. We have to bring about the most radical revolution in the people's traditional ideas of the relation between ruler and ruled, and it will be a difficult and even dangerous business, for it is neither safe nor easy to meddle with traditional ideas in India. Unless the political changes now in contemplation are accompanied by an educational campaign directed to awaking in all classes alike, but especially in this particular class, a sense of citizenship, disaster will certainly result' (from an official report quoted without dissent in the Montagu-Chelmsford Report, paragraph 137, p. 113).

III.

'It would be a disaster for India to be forced into the narrow form of constitutionalism that developed, with its essential condition of two great rival parties, in England through historical and natural causes, but is now confessedly in need of reform. . . . Constitutional government has succeeded only where it has been cast in a form natural to the history and development of the people. . . . Why should India be

**forced to imitate a** system of government evolved through many centuries in a geographically small country with two historical parties? . . . We want self-government, we want responsible government in the widest sense of the term—that of ultimate responsibility to the people—but **we do not want our nascent national institutions to be put into swaddling clothes, because one word** [*scil.* "**responsible**"] **instead of another** [*scil.* "**self-**"] **was chosen by the British War Cabinet for its public declaration**' (His Highness the Aga Khan, *India in Transition*: Philip Lee Warner, London, 1918, pp. 165, 166).

N.B.—The thick type is not in the originals.

# CONTENTS

# CHAPTER 1

## THE GENESIS AND AUTHORITY OF THE 'PRONOUNCEMENT' OF AUGUST 20, 1917

**Need of discussion.** The authors of the *Report on Indian Constitutional Reform (1918)*, cited as 'the Report', declare that 'in a matter of so great intricacy and importance it is obvious that full and public discussion is necessary'. That declaration, which looks so frank, appears from various indications to be really subject in the minds of its authors to the limitation that the discussion should be restricted to details, while the main theorems of the document should not be disputed. The Report purports to set forth a highly complicated plan devised in pursuance of the 'pronouncement' of August 20, 1917, to which a sort of sacrosanct character is ascribed by Mr. Montagu. His unusual and rather unconstitutional procedure actually has succeeded in giving his utterance an importance beyond its intrinsic merits.

**Plan of this essay.** It will be convenient in the first place to reprint the text of the 'pronouncement'; next, to examine the story of its genesis, so far as revealed, and then to discuss the extent to which the promises made by His Majesty's Government on August 20, 1917, are binding on succeeding Governments, on Parliament, or on the nation. The consideration of those matters involves the question of the interpretation of the pledge given by the War Cabinet. When those preliminary discussions have been disposed of in this chapter, the next three chapters will be devoted to the frank historical statement of certain Indian peculiarities which condition all possible reforms. The fifth chapter collects certain rhetorical passages in the Report which are in most obvious conflict with realities. The sixth chapter gives a summary of the concrete proposals put forth by the authors of the Report and other writers. That summary is followed by a critical discussion, and the essay is concluded by an attempt to assemble various constructive suggestions which seem to be practicable.

**The 'Pronouncement'.** The text of the 'pronouncement' of August 20, 1917, is:

'The policy of His Majesty's Government, with which the Government of India are in complete accord, is that of increasing the association of Indians in every branch of the administration and the gradual development of self-governing institutions with a view to the progressive realization of responsible government in India, as an integral part of the British Empire.

'They have decided that substantial steps in this direction should be taken as soon as possible, and that it is of the highest importance, as a preliminary to considering what these steps should be, that there should be a free and informal exchange of opinion between those in authority at Home and in India. His Majesty's Government have accordingly decided, with His Majesty's approval, that I should accept the Viceroy's invitation to proceed to India to discuss these matters with the Viceroy and the Government of India, to consider with the Viceroy the views of Local Governments, and to receive the suggestions of representative bodies and others. I would add that progress in this policy can only be achieved by successive stages. The British Government and the Government of India, on whom the responsibility lies for the welfare and advancement of the Indian peoples, must be judges of the time and measure of each advance, and they must be guided by the co-operation received from those upon whom new opportunities of Service will thus be conferred and by the extent to which it is found that confidence can be reposed in their sense of responsibility. Ample opportunity will be afforded for the public discussion of the proposals, which will be submitted in due course to Parliament.'

**Its origin.** We cannot expect to obtain access to the recent confidential correspondence between the Government of India and the Secretary of State. Failing that, we must fall back upon the authoritative statement made by Lord Curzon of Kedleston in the House of Lords on October 24, 1918. His lordship explained the genesis of the 'pronouncement' in these words, according to the report in *The Times*:

'That announcement was the result of prolonged correspondence with the Government of India, of close and repeated examination at home, and of an amount of labour which must have rarely been expended upon a public announcement. I imagine that as much care was devoted to the declaration, perhaps more than to the famous declaration of Her Majesty Queen Victoria in 1858—a declaration which, if I remember rightly, was framed by Lord Derby and corrected and amended by Her Majesty's own hand.

'Without claiming for a moment that this announcement was therefore invested with a pontifical character, it had a seriousness and intended weight which your lordships would not dispute.

'Lord Crewe has said that the declaration no doubt sprang from the circumstances of the war. I can quite believe that had the war not occurred the declaration would not have been made either in that particular form or at that particular time. The war has altered the whole atmosphere of life, and it is inconceivable that it should have passed through its tragic course without leaving much more than a ripple upon the surface of the Indian nation and without stirring its depths.'

Lord Curzon's exposition is elucidated by a passage in the Report (paragraph 287), which records that

'meanwhile the difficulties of administration in India were rapidly increasing. Lord Chelmsford's Government felt that without the declaration of policy for which they were pressing, it was impossible for them to act effectively on a directed course. The announcement of August 20 cleared the situation, and was hailed with almost as much relief by the authorities as satisfaction by the politicians.'

The matter has been carried somewhat further by the

joint declaration of the Prime Minister and Mr. Bonar Law published on November 22, 1918, that

'the Cabinet has already defined in unmistakable language the goal of British policy in India to be the development of responsible government by gradual stages. To the general terms of that declaration we adhere and propose to give effect.'

That ministerial announcement did not interest the constituencies or influence the tenure of a single seat at the election held on December 14, 1918.

By putting together all the official statements we learn that the 'pronouncement' originated in the administrative difficulties of the Government of India during the war; that it was intended to afford 'satisfaction to the politicians'; that its phraseology was decided after prolonged correspondence with India and repeated consultations in London; that the substance of the declaration, although not invested with a 'pontifical character', is a serious programme of Cabinet policy, accepted in its 'general terms'; and that the Cabinet now in office, which is likely to remain in power, intends to give effect to its declared policy. Lord Curzon's language, while somewhat modifying Mr. Montagu's rhetoric, cannot have much effect in sobering the extravagant hopes raised by previous overstatement of the intentions and aims of the Government. The terms 'self-government' and 'responsible government' were not defined in the course of the debate in the House of Lords. Their meaning will be analysed in Chapter 7 of this essay.

**Mode of enunciation.** The 'pronouncement', which the Secretary of State describes in grandiose style as 'the most momentous utterance ever made in India's chequered history', was given to the world in a curiously unpretentious way, as if its authors desired to avoid notice. Some private member asked a question about Mr. Montagu's intended tour, and received in answer 'the most momentous utterance'. At that time the House of Commons was tired, the session was drawing to a close, and the minds of all men were absorbed in the war. The statement aroused no interest in the British public, and remained practically unnoticed in England. If such hiding of the light was intentional, the device succeeded completely. The reception of the 'pronouncement' in India was very different. As we have seen, it was instantly welcomed with effusion by both Lord Chelmsford and the 'politicians'. All of them proceeded to make the most of the 'clarion call', also described as 'the greatest landmark in the history of India'. Expectations of the agitating classes were raised to the highest pitch, and great pains were taken to establish the answer to a question as amounting to a formal engagement, binding not only on the Cabinet which gave the answer, but on all succeeding ministries, on Parliament, and even on the constituencies which had never heard of the matter. Mr. Curtis went so far as to declare that because the ministerial answer to a question on an Indian subject failed to provoke a vote of censure, that is 'equivalent to its acceptance by the Imperial Parliament and electorate'.

**The authority of the 'pronouncement'.** Never before has the answer to a question in the House had to carry such a weight of alleged authority. As Sir Harry Stephen correctly argues, 'according to all precedent Mr. Montagu's "pronouncement" bound no one outside the Government, and was as far from being a national promise as are the contents of a King's Speech'. That exposition of the constitutional position is still, in December, 1918, strictly accurate. The utterance means no more than that the existing Cabinet, if it remains in power, is bound to introduce an India Bill drawn in accordance with the 'general terms' of the answer given on August 20, 1917.

But dexterous pulling of the strings in India has modified the actual situation by deliberate exaggeration of the significance of the 'pronouncement', which, as already mentioned, has been worked so as to encourage aspirations and raise expectations which cannot possibly be gratified. The authorities who have countenanced such exaggeration have assumed a grave responsibility, and have laid themselves open to the suspicion of trying to prejudge the issue before it can be submitted to Parliament in constitutional form. The tortuous procedure adopted justifies Sir Harry Stephen in saying that the Secretary of State has managed to 'deal a blow at Parliamentary Government in England while preparing the way for Responsible Government in India'. In consequence of the methods employed by Mr. Montagu it has been impossible to raise a direct issue in Parliament. All the reformers in India seem to be persuaded that both Houses of Parliament stand fully committed not only to the exact terms of the 'pronouncement' as an inspired oracle, but also to the main proposals of the Report. As a matter of fact, that Report binds nobody, and has not even been considered by the Cabinet (December, 1918). The Under Secretary of State declared officially in the House of Lords in October that the scheme elaborated in the Report 'does not necessarily commit the Government nor the country'. Notwithstanding that explicit declaration it is clear that strenuous efforts are being made in India to treat the recommendations of Mr. Montagu and Lord Chelmsford as almost equivalent to an Act of Parliament, subject only to amendment in minor details.

The machinations to prejudge the questions at issue, and to represent them as decided long before even the drafting of a Bill, much less its passing, deserve the severe language which has been applied to them.

**Unfettered debate.** The 'pronouncement' and the Report, when completed, must be read and debated together. They cannot be separated, and neither has any claim to be regarded as a *chose jugée*. Parliament and the public should not be juggled out of their right to free, unfettered discussion of both principles and details. No minister is entitled to gag debate in advance. Debate must not be 'cabin'd, cribb'd, confin'd' by any formula. The omnipotence of Parliament in matters political being unquestioned, and the authority of an Act of Parliament being supreme, the highest interests of both India and England require that the decision in this matter, which will really be 'momentous', should be based on the fullest possible knowledge, formed after exhaustive debate, and free, so far as human infirmity permits, from the stain of party spirit.

The authors of the Report, while well aware of the penalty involved in failure, profess to believe that their plans must succeed merely because Mr. Montagu and Lord Chelmsford desire that they should. A spirit of credulous and yet frightened optimism disfigures the whole Report. As Lord Sydenham of Combe justly observes, 'they absolutely admit the most striking facts opposed to their notions, and then ignore those facts when they come to make concrete proposals'.

# CHAPTER 2

## THE HISTORICAL INDIAN IDEAL OF GOVERNMENT

**Vedic folk-motes.** Popular assemblies, with functions like those of the Homeric *agora* or the modern Afghan *jirga*, decided the affairs of the small Indo-Aryan tribes in remote Vedic times, thousands of years ago. When the caste system gradually developed, impairing the unity of the people, and tribal organization was largely replaced by territorial kingdoms, the royal power necessarily increased, and the expression of the public will by general assemblies became impossible. No Indian institution in historical times can be traced back to the Vedic folk-motes.

**Kingless nations.** Long afterwards, at the time of Alexander's invasion in the fourth century B.C., and down to about the fifth century of the Christian era, we hear of sundry peoples or nations in Northern India who enjoyed forms of republican government. Little is on record concerning details, but, so far as is known, the republics seem to have been usually under the rule of oligarchies. The Licchavis of Tirhūt, one of the most famous of the republican peoples, almost certainly were Mongolian hill-men akin to the Gūrkhas and Tibetans. Perhaps all the kingless nations belonged to the same category. However that may be, all the popular or oligarchical constitutions faded away, without leaving any mark on the general course of Indian history.

**Statecraft.** The theory and practice of government have been favourite subjects with Hindu authors for much more than two millenniums. The earliest extant treatise, composed in the fourth century B.C., avowedly is based upon a long series of lost works, some of which must have been at least two or three centuries prior in date. Kautilya, the author of the most ancient book known, makes merely a passing allusion to the kingless nations, and devotes his text to the elaboration of the theory and practice of monarchy. Many later writers continued the discussion of the same subject.

**The King.** All authors agree in representing as the centre and mainspring of the body politic the King or Rājā, who was often appointed in early times by some kind of election. The principle of hereditary succession gradually grew in strength, and, as a rule, the royal authority was transmitted from father to son, as long as a dynasty lasted.

The King, however appointed, invariably enjoyed autocratic powers. If a Hindu, he was supposed to follow the counsels of wise ministers and reverend Brahmans offered in accordance with the sacred scriptures. If a Muhammadan, he was supposed similarly to owe allegiance to Koranic law and tradition. But in practice a masterful king was always able to free himself from the trammels of law, subject to the risks of revolt, dethronement, and death. History tells of many such monarchs. Akbar, who had ceased to be a Musalman during the last twenty-three years of his life, is the most conspicuous instance. No form of government except the autocratic was recognized as being suitable to Indian conditions. Akbar's able and learned secretary emphatically affirmed that autocracy was the only known remedy for a world of confusion and hornets, and, as a matter of fact, no materials for the construction of any other system of government then existed. Sivājī the Marāthā, in the latter part of the seventeenth century, always retained supreme power in his own hands, although he consulted an organized cabinet of ministers and was deferential to Brahmans from religious motives. The decadent rulers of the eighteenth century preserved the tradition of autocracy, which was the sole form of government in India when the British entered on the scene. The autocracy, which even Mr. Montagu and Lord Chelmsford desire to preserve for the Government of India (*Report*, p. 231), has a long history.

**Duties of the King.** Both Hindus and Muhammadans recognized that the King had duties as well as rights, and that if he was from one point of view the master, he was from another the servant of the State. A recent Hindu author justly observes that 'the conception of the King as servant of the State was one of the basic principles of political thought in Ancient India'. The idea finds frequent expression in literature, most emphatically, perhaps, in the declarations of Asoka. That idea led to the corollary that the ideal monarch should work hard and freely sacrifice his personal convenience for the benefit of his people, whom he should regard as his children. The parental relation involved the necessity of chastisement when the children misbehaved.

**A strong executive.** Authors of text-books and unanimous public opinion were agreed that the executive must justify its existence by being strong. The art of government was compendiously described as being the Law of Punishment (*Dandanīti*), and the books are full of admonitions to the King to use his vast powers firmly, justly, and impartially, without undue tenderness to the evil-doer. Saith Manu:

'Dread of the rod alone restrains the bad,
Controls the good, and makes a nation happy . . .
The King must therefore punish fearlessly;
Else would the strong oppress the weak . . .
That King is equally unjust who frees
The guilty or condemns the innocent' (Monier Williams).

**Stern justice.** Popular resentment was not aroused by the infliction of cruel penalties, provided that they were imposed impartially without respect of persons. In the seventeenth century, Jahāngīr, whose sentences showed appalling ferocity, was reputed a just ruler, because he never spared a prince more than a peasant. Aurangzēb, on the other hand, while admired for his religious devotion, was condemned as a sovereign because, 'from reverence for the injunctions of the Law, he did not make use of punishment, and without punishment the administration of a country cannot be maintained'.

The small and influential class commonly described as 'educated India' has, as we all know, very different ideas of government.

**Indian tradition.** But it is important for even advanced reformers to remember that their notions run counter to a deep stream of Indian tradition which has been flowing for thousands of years. Ninety-nine out of a hundred Indians, whether Hindus or Muhammadans, cherish as their ideal of government that of the virtuous Rājā, who works hard, is easily accessible, is sternly and impartially just, yet loves his people as a father loves his children, and is guided by the advice of wise ministers based upon immemorial tradition. Executive weakness, unjust partiality, and departure from tradition are regarded with substantial unanimity as among the worst possible faults of a government.

**Personal government.** The ordinary men and women of India do not understand impersonal government. Talk about elective councils and 'diarchies' is as unintelligible to them as the binomial theorem. They crave for government by a person to whom they can render loyal homage, which easily passes into worship. That craving is gratified in the Native or Protected States, where every subject knows who his ruler is. Even a ruler whom European criticism may condemn often enjoys the obedient loyalty of his people.

**The Crown and India.** The history of British India and the peculiar relations of the Indian governments with the democracy of Great Britain forbid the full realization of the popular Indian ideal in these times. But the now acknowledged supremacy of the Crown offers an opportunity for the exhibition of the traditional Indian loyalty to a person, which should be sedulously kept open. The Indian people have enjoyed the privilege of seeing face to face their King-Emperor, the successor of Rāma, Asoka, and Akbar. Their heartfelt loyalty should not be quenched by the cold water of democratic theory. Mr. Lovat Fraser truly remarks that

> 'the Crown has become the link to which his subjects in every clime readily attach themselves; and the King's journey symbolizes the inauguration of a new era. It demonstrates to the whole world the reality and solidity of British rule in India, deriving as it does its main strength, not from the force of arms, but from the loyal acquiescence of princes and peoples in the supremacy of a British monarch.'

As I have said elsewhere, 'the intense and profound emotion which greeted the Sovereign and his gracious consort was the spontaneous, heartfelt offering of India to their royal persons'. An eyewitness felt that the solemn assembly at Delhi was 'the ultimate expression of the potent force of kingship, which in that resplendent scene reached a height we may never see again'.

A real danger exists that the influence of that 'potent force' may be whittled away by embittered controversy between Extremists, Moderates, and the rest, or smothered in the smoke of deplorable racial jealousies.

**Antiquity of tradition.** Reformers are apt to forget the immeasurable antiquity of Indian tradition. The ancient scriptures are neither obsolete nor dead. They still express the inmost thoughts of the voiceless myriads of to-day as truly as they record the sentiments of their ancestors in the distant past. No passing wind of doctrine can shake the rock of Indian tradition. The shadows flee away, the wall remains. The fly on the rim buzzes for a moment, the wheel of life rolls on. Truly, 'it is neither safe nor easy to meddle with traditional ideas in India'.

**The King-Emperor.** One of the gravest defects in the Report is its failure to say a word about the King-Emperor or to show the slightest appreciation of the immense political value of the loyal homage to his person which all ranks in India are eager and proud to tender. That willing loyalty, if fitly recognized, will go far to neutralize the disjunctive effects of the differences in race, religion, language, caste, and customs on which an historical survey of the possibilities of Indian Reform necessarily lays stress. Many years ago, in 1899, Sir Theodore Morison recorded the just observation that 'if a great statesman ever had the opportunity of constructing the whole edifice of government afresh, he would assuredly seize upon the loyalty of the people to the Queen as the cardinal fact upon which to found the fabric of Empire; he would recognize that the Queen is beyond all comparison the greatest political force in India' (*Imperial Rule in India*, p. 53).

**The 'golden link'.** Although it may not be 'impossible', as Thucydides suggested it to be, for a democracy to rule an empire, the undertaking undoubtedly is difficult. The difficulty is not insuperable, and the necessary co-operation of the full-grown British democracy with the Indian peoples steeped in monarchical tradition can be best achieved by using to the utmost practicable extent the golden link of the Crown. To quote the language of the Prime Minister: 'If Parliament rise to its great opportunities, then the Empire and the Throne—which has won added respect, stability, and lustre through the action of its occupant during these trying times—will be firmly established on the only solid basis, that of a happy, a prosperous, and a contented people.'

The Aga Khan, who sees a vision of a great South Asiatic Federation headed by a regenerated India, is right when he says that 'happily the Imperial Crown provides the venerated centre round which the great States of the Empire can unite'.

Whether that vision of a Federation be ever realized or not, methods certainly can be devised which will preserve the inestimable sentiments of loyalty to and affection for the Sovereign felt by all classes of the Indian population, and will do much to bind India and England together in a real union destined to last for centuries.

But the methods for attaining that end are not exactly those of the Report.

# CHAPTER 3

## DIVERSITY AND CONFLICTS OF RACES AND RELIGIONS

**Conflict of races and religions.** India has been the battle-ground of races and religions from time immemorial. The conflict is not yet ended, and it is impossible for statesmen to make wise provision for government at the present day unless they realize vividly the secular duration of such conflict, the persistence of ancient feuds for centuries, and the extreme difficulty of preserving the peace.

**Smothered fires.** Somebody is certain to argue that at a time when the Moslem League is co-operating with the National Congress, when many indications point to a growing sentiment in favour of unification, and sanguine hopes are expressed that ancient animosities may disappear, so that all sections of the Indian population may be welded into one great nation, it is not right to rip up old sores or to remind people of the existence of bitter hostility between different classes of the population. Unhappily the truth is that sanguine anticipations of the early realization of a common political identity are not justified either by the facts of history or by observation of present conditions. The old sores still fester, the smothered fires still smoulder, and the superficial appearance of unity is delusive. Silence about facts does not alter the facts. Statesmanship is concerned with what is, not with what ought to be. Nothing is gained in the end by prophesying smooth things or evading the frank recognition of unwelcome realities. Idealist reformers, including the authors of the Report, display a marked tendency to dispose of such realities by a few slight passing allusions and to indulge in aspirations for improvement wholly unwarranted by the facts. If the rulers of India shut their eyes and make believe that all is well when it is not well, the realities of the situation will assert themselves, with results disastrous to all concerned.

**Misfits.** Lord Bryce observes concerning the majority of the South American republics so called that 'the constitutions did not suit the facts, and the facts had to prevail against the constitutions'. It seems to me that India is in imminent danger of being clothed with a constitution which does not fit the facts, and that the task of stating in plain language the historical record and the actual conditions demanding extreme caution should be undertaken with the purpose of helping Parliament, the final arbiter, to find the best solution of an exceedingly complex problem.

**Survivals.** Far away in the dim past we can discern the early stages of the armed conflict between the immigrant Indo-Aryan tribes and the indigenous inhabitants of the country, Dravidians and others, as well as the prolonged and still unfinished contest between the ideas of Brahmanical Hinduism and those of the aboriginal religions. The Indo-Aryan victory seems at first sight to be complete both on the battle-field and in the world of ideas, but closer scrutiny reveals the survival of many notions, practices, and customs, alien and hostile to Brahmanical thought and feeling. If all reference to Islam, Christianity, and other foreign religions be put aside for a moment, it may be said that India, excepting uncultured tribes, is essentially Hindu, the land of the Brahmans. The unity underlying the obvious diversity of India may be summed up in the word Hinduism.

The modern Hindu revival, the fruit in no small measure of the labours of European scholarship, tends to increase the sentiment striving for political unification, which undoubtedly is a living and potent force. Nevertheless, an immense mass of pre-Hindu beliefs and practices continues to exist. The religious unity even of Hindu India is so far from complete that opportunities for conflict abound, and form a serious obstacle to political unification.

**Various national types.** The diversity of the Indian peoples is apparent to the most casual observer. 'L'Inde est un monde,' as a French author neatly expresses the fact. Although in India, as in other lands, much commingling of blood has taken place, in spite of caste restrictions, the national types of the various peoples persist. The Tamils, Marāthās, Bengālīs, and Rājpūts, to name but a few, have each their distinct histories, traditions, and customs.

While Hindu India possesses a single sacred language, the Sanskrit, which is a powerful factor in the incomplete unity of Hinduism, the number of vernacular languages and dialects is almost past counting. That diversity of speech implies deep divergence in ideas, and history teaches that such divergence going back for millenniums is an almost insurmountable barrier against close union, political or social.

The attractive vision of a League of Nations binding together the peoples of Europe, or even those of the whole world, in an alliance consecrated to perpetual peace is admittedly difficult of realization. The welding together of all the peoples of Hind into one great Indian nation is little less difficult.

Throughout the ages, until a century ago, when the British peace was imposed with general assent, we find India divided among the diverse races, usually hostile one to the other, and consequently parcelled into innumerable unstable states continually at war. The great settlement of 1818 cast oil upon the waters and stilled the storm. But the waves still heave and swell. The forces which wrecked society in the eighteenth century are still working only a little way below the surface.

It seems advisable to illustrate such general reflections by citing a few historical instances of racial and religious conflict which suggest lessons applicable to the problems of to-day.

**Tolerance the rule.** Indians justly pride themselves on the assertion that religious opinion in their land is free, and that most indigenous rulers have shown statesmanlike tolerance for all creeds. Ordinarily persecution did not occur, and adherents of different religions managed to live together peaceably.

**Persecution of Jains.** But from time to time severe persecutions deliberately carried out by kings have occurred and are on record. Jainism, which was the dominant religion in the peninsula for about a thousand years, but is now almost non-existent in that region, seems to have owed its decay largely to systematic persecution. At Madura, in the seventh century, a king who had been converted by his wife from Jainism to the Brahmanical Saiva faith, persecuted his former co-religionists with such savage fury that he executed no less than eight thousand of them by the slow torture of impalement. The atrocity is commemorated not only by certain paintings on the walls of the Madura temple and sculptures elsewhere, but, as a Hindu scholar (Mr. T. A. Gopinatha Rao) informs us, by a festival (*utsava*) still celebrated at Madura under the name of the 'impalement of the Jains'. Even after twelve centuries the local sectarian rancour is so bitter that the anniversary of the cruel execution is regarded by orthodox Hindus as a proper occasion for festivities. In Northern India riots have been often occasioned by the public performance of Jain ceremonies.

**Fights of devotees.** Fierce fights between rival Hindu sects, especially between bodies of fakeers or devotees, used to be common, and were not interfered with by the authorities.

On one occasion of such a fight at Thānēsar, Akbar, so far from interfering, sent some of his own soldiers to join in the fray, until about a thousand men were engaged and a score killed. He regarded the affair as good sport. Similar conflicts on a scale even larger continued to occur in the eighteenth century.

At Hardwār in 1760, 'on the great bathing day, the rival mobs of *gosains* and *bairāgīs* had a long battle, in which 1,800 men are said to have perished. In 1795 the Sikh pilgrims slew 500 of the *gosains*.' Improved police arrangements now forbid the occurrence of such catastrophes. But the spirit which caused them is as rampant as ever, and any laxity in the highly skilled and elaborately organized control now exercised by European officers would inevitably result in a repetition of the old-fashioned scenes of bloodshed.

**Religion exploited.** Grievances absolutely unconnected with religion are often exploited by agitators and utilized as pretexts for inflaming the fanaticism of the mob, which is easily led to regard an unpopular innovation by casteless and ceremonially impure rulers as being an intentional outrage on religious sentiments. Thus, at Bareilly in Rohilkhand, in 1816, a proposal to introduce a house-tax for municipal purposes was misrepresented in that way and was made the occasion for an outbreak which cost more than 300 lives. A still more conspicuous example of the method is afforded by the Travancore rebellion of 1808, when an astute minister named Velu Tampi, who had political disputes with the Resident, used them as the text for an inflammatory proclamation which set the whole State on fire by persuading the people that their religion and caste were in danger, although, as a matter of fact, neither was threatened in any way. A Hindu author tells us that 'the whole country rose like one man. Their religious susceptibilities were touched, which in a conservative country like Travancore is like smoking in a powder magazine.'

The rebels immediately murdered thirty European soldiers in cold blood. When encountered by a large force of regular troops they fought a battle in which they lost 700 killed. Yet there was not the shadow of justification for the minister's cunning appeal to the religious feelings of the peasantry. The application of those cases to present-day conditions is not far to seek. Modern anarchists know how to improve on the old-fashioned crude methods for exploiting fanaticism and make use of scientifically planned organization. The confession of Barindra Kumar Ghosh, recorded in the *Rowlatt Commission Report*, contains the words:

> 'I returned to Bengal convinced that a purely political propaganda would not do for the country and that people must be trained up spiritually to face dangers. . . . As I thought that some people of India would not be made to do any work except through religion, I wanted, &c.'

The result was a long series of murders and gang robberies committed by young enthusiasts who believed their crimes to be justified or even demanded by their religion.

**Dangerous agitation.** The masses invariably translate political propaganda into terms which they can understand. The highly organized political agitation carried on in villages and small towns for the last four years, as described in the *Manchester Guardian* special number of March 28, 1918 (pp. 32–3), must produce a formidable outburst of racial and religious animosity. The evidence indicates that such animosity has been grievously inflamed already, and might easily become uncontrollable.

**Hindus and Muslims.** The extreme ferocity displayed by the Muhammadan armies for centuries, and constantly approved by Muslim chroniclers, is well known to all students of Indian history. The Hindus retaliated with equal violence on the rare occasions when they got the chance. Those long-past horrors are not forgotten, nor can it be said truly that the spirit which caused them is dead. I sleeps, but is very easily aroused by some trivial incident, as all magistrates know. The joint acceptance in December, 1916, of a scheme of reform by the Congress and the All-India Moslem League is far from having 'solved the greatest internal problem which India had', as Mr. Jinnah boldly claims that it did. Sores ten centuries old are not so easily healed. While everything that tends to bridge over the gulf between Hindu and Muslim is to be welcomed, the wise man will hesitate before he accepts a frail thread as a solid bridge. The All-India Moslem League, the organ of a few lawyers, mostly of the Shia sect, does not represent the 66½ millions of Indian Muhammadans, many of whom have repudiated it. Serious Hindu and Muhammadan riots in modern times have been innumerable.

**Benares, Bombay, and Bihar.** One of the most notable outbreaks occurred at Benares in 1809, when one half of the population was armed against the other and the rival mobs were excited to demoniac passion. The Bombay riots of 1893 were equally grave. The Hindu attack on the Musalman villages of the Patna, Gaya, and Shahabad or Arrah districts in Bihar in 1917 was the most formidable outbreak of the kind recorded, so far as I know. The special Court of Commissioners declared in December of that year that 'these disturbances were the result of a deliberately planned and widely extended conspiracy in the [Shahabad] district to loot, terrorize, and crush the Muhammadan minority'. More than a hundred villages in the Shahabad district alone were plundered, and many scores of respectable Muhammadan women were stripped naked and put to open shame. The leaders in the disgraceful attacks were men of good local position and considerable education. These crimes occurred *after* the adhesion of the All-India Moslem League to the Congress programme. The Report barely alludes to those organized outrages which have been justly described as the Bihar or Arrah War. During the autumn of 1918 Hindu-Muhammadan conflicts on a large scale, attended with considerable bloodshed, have occurred in Calcutta and near Hardwār.

# CHAPTER 4

## CASTE AND CASTE DISPUTES

**The mystery of caste.** 'India', as Dr. John Wilson truly observed, 'is emphatically the land of mystery. It has been a land of mystery to distant strangers, to friendly and hostile visitors, and even to its own inhabitants.' The greatest Indian mystery is the institution known to modern writers as Caste.

The Report displays inadequate recognition of the existence and significance of that mystery, which is referred to by mere passing allusions in five passages only (paras. 132, 140, 149, 152, and 228). As Sir Harry Stephen truly observes, 'how Responsible Government is to be adapted to Caste the Report does not say'. The passage in para. 149 (page 123), which speaks of 'everything that breaks down the barriers between communities, and makes men regard each other as neighbours and not as the wearers of some caste or creed insignia, hastens on the day when self-government within the Empire will be attained', betrays an inability to conceive the real nature of the institution. It would be unreasonable to expect that the authors should be able to master the inner nature of Indian society, to which their European experience offers no parallel. Nobody even moderately well informed on the subject could use the language quoted, which implies that caste is contemplated by the authors as a thing external capable of being laid aside. The caste of an Indian is *not* to him a matter of insignia to be worn or doffed at pleasure. It is bone of his bone and flesh of his flesh.

**Caste facts.** Apart from the deficiencies of the Report, which are of the kind to be expected, it is absolutely necessary that politicians who dream of an Indian democracy should at least try to realize what caste means. Caste is peculiar to India, the analogies or resemblances of institutions in other countries being faint and remote. If the politicians fail to recognize the extent to which that peculiar institution stands in their way, they must fail in their attempt to democratize India, because the facts are so strong that even an Act of Parliament, or a dozen Acts of Parliament, cannot shake them. The fact of caste must be faced boldly and without evasion by every would-be reformer.

**Magnitude.** In the first place it is essential to visualize the magnitude of the institution. The Indian population which may be classed fairly as Hindus, bound by the laws of caste, numbers considerably more than 200 millions.

Although nothing could be more inconsistent with the spirit of Islam than is the exclusive caste system, Indian Muhammadans, numbering about 66½ millions, have been so largely infected by their Hindu environment that, if the majority of them be included, we may affirm with confidence that at least 250 millions of people, amounting to about one-sixth of the estimated population of the world, are held firmly in the trammels of caste.

**±3,000 castes.** Those 250 millions are divided into about 3,000 castes, or water-tight social compartments, without reckoning innumerable sub-castes. Although the exact number of existing castes cannot be determined, for reasons too complex for exposition in this place, it is certainly true that in the year 1918 the castes in existence must be about 3,000, more or less, as estimated by Ketkar. The precise figure does not matter. It would be a figure of that order, if it could be ascertained.

What, then, do we mean by saying that Indian society is broken up into some 3,000 castes?

In order to answer that question we must form a clear notion of what we mean by 'a caste' and by 'the caste institution'.

**Definition of caste.** The word caste (*casta*) is Portuguese; the thing is so peculiarly Indian that it separates India from the rest of the world far more impassably than deserts, seas, or mountains. A good working definition of the institution is given by Sir Charles Gough, who states that 'caste may be generally described as the theory and practice of hereditary social distinctions carried to the extremest limits and confirmed by the sanctions of religion'.

An elementary fact often forgotten is that in India the unit of society is the family, not the individual as in modern England. Remembering that fundamental proposition, we may define 'a caste' as being 'a group of families internally united by peculiar rules for the hereditary observance of ceremonial purity, especially in the matters of diet and marriage'.

The same rules fence off the group from all other similar groups, each of which is regulated by its own inherited customs.

**New castes.** In modern times it is impossible for any person or family to be transferred from one caste to another. New castes may and not infrequently do spring up in various ways, but every individual and family must ordinarily remain in the caste as determined by birth. In the cases where caste is lost by breach of the rules, the seceders may found a new caste. Hindu opinion, for instance, regards communities of Christian converts as such new castes. In spite of the efforts of missionaries, who for many years past have been almost unanimous in requiring converts to break their old caste, experience shows that it is usually impossible for converts, whether won individually or by 'mass movements', to renounce the idea of caste, which is in their blood. The sentiment continually crops up in one form or another.

**Muhammadan castes.** The Indian Muhammadans, in so far as they are descended from Hindu converts, similarly retain their ancient caste organization and continue to be saturated with the notions of their remote ancestors. Few Muslims in India, whatever be their origin, are able to keep themselves quite free from caste prejudices. For example, they are, as a rule, unwilling to eat with Europeans, as Turks, Persians, and Arabs freely do.

**Caste species.** The Hindus have not any name for the caste institution because they regard it as an essential part of the divine order of nature. It is out of the question for a Hindu to think of himself otherwise than as a member of some particular caste or species of Hindu mankind. He calls a caste *jāt*, which means 'species'. The families making up the *jāt* are not necessarily descended from a common ancestor, and, in Northern India at all events, rarely are so descended. Caste in the north is not very largely concerned with race, meaning descent. The castes of the Peninsula, on the other hand, may be generally described as petrified tribes.

Although community of occupation is the basis of some castes, many admit of great occupational variety. Each caste community becomes in practice a distinct species, whoever the ancestors may have been, and whether the lawful occupations pursued by its members be few or many. The distinctness of the species rests upon the effective operation of its rules for the preservation of ceremonial purity in diet and marriage.

**Dominance of caste.** No Indian can escape from the influence of the caste idea, which is 'the soul as well as the body of Hinduism'. A Hindu author lays down the propositions, which are true and supported by general opinion, that it is by means of caste distinctions that the Hindu religion has been so well preserved; they are the chief support of that religion, and when they give way there can be no doubt that the Hindu religion will perish. Hinduism is primarily an extremely ancient social system based upon and inseparable from the caste institution, which is regarded as being of divine origin. That system assumes and presupposes as a divinely revealed axiom the congenital and eternal distinction and inequality of the different groups. Whatever may happen, the Brahman must remain at the top of the structure, fed, cherished, protected, and honoured by his inferiors, that is to say, by everybody else, be he prince or peasant.

**Unity of Hinduism.** Nearly all Hindus agree in venerating Brahmans, in professing obedience to certain sacred scriptures, in honouring certain major deities, in respecting the sanctity of cows, in reverencing the same holy places, and so on.

In that sense Hinduism may be called a religion as well as a social system. The Indian religious traditions preserved and the modes of worship practised from the Himalaya to Cape Comorin have sufficient features in common to warrant Hindus in feeling conscious of a considerable degree of religious unity as against the rest of the world.

**No Hindu creed.** But Hinduism is not a religion in the sense that either Christianity or Islam is. It has no prophet-founder and no creed. It is merely the social and religious expression of the Hindu ideal of duty (*dharma*) as developed during the course of several millenniums.

No Hindu is required to obey any one prophet or to confess to any particular creed. So long as he eats the diet and marries the woman prescribed by the rules of the caste into which he was born, he may believe or disbelieve what he pleases.

**Caste ethics.** The text-books, while recognizing certain elementary virtues as binding upon all men, are emphatic in asserting that each group of castes has special duties and morals of its own. Individual castes often have each their own standard of duty. What is right for one caste or group of castes may be quite wrong for another caste or group. That principle rests upon the abstract doctrines of Hindu philosophy about rebirth, &c., which cannot be discussed in this place. The practical result is that Hinduism recognizes many conflicting moral standards or codes of ethics, because the members of each caste or group of kindred castes look to the public opinion only of their own caste-fellows, which is not necessarily in accordance with the Ten Commandments or any other statement of universal moral law. When the special caste conception of duty (*dharma*) comes into conflict with the general moral law, the caste duty prevails. That is the explanation of Thuggee, temple prostitution, and various other forms of crime or immorality, organized either on a caste basis or on an analogous system. The Thug stranglers were convinced that they worked with divine sanction under the protection of a goddess, and were never troubled by remorse because the practices sanctioned by their brotherhood conflicted glaringly with ordinary morality. Ordinary Hindus often acquiesced in that view and were willing and ready to protect the Thugs. Other examples might be cited. Those observations have a direct bearing upon all attempts to form an Indian nationality, not to speak of an Indian democracy. A population broken up into sections differing not only in blood, language, social customs, and creed, but also in their ideas of morality, does not readily coalesce into a political unity. Such coalescence, if ever attained, must be deferred to a distant future.

**A guiding principle.** 'Caste interferes, in short, with all the relations and events of life, and with what precedes or follows, or what is supposed to precede and follow life. It reigns supreme in the innumerable classes and divisions of the Hindus, whether they originate in family descent, in religious opinions, in civil or sacred occupations, or in local residence; and it professes to regulate all their interests, affairs, and relationships. Caste is the guiding principle of each of the classes and divisions of the Hindus viewed in their distinct or associated capacity' (J. Wilson).

'Custom', as Manu lays down, 'is the highest *dharma*', or 'transcendent law of duty'. Immemorial custom fortified by revelation is the basis of caste. The institution, with roots fastened securely in the prehistoric past and accepted as an essential element in the divine ordering of the world, is reverenced alike by the superiors who command and by the inferiors who obey.

So ineradicable is the idea of caste that the lowest ranks of society, the sweepers, scavengers, and others who perform the basest offices, and are regarded as standing outside the pale of Hinduism, have formed caste organizations of their own, quite independent of those recognized by Hindu tradition. Such 'outcaste castes', to use an unavoidably paradoxical term, govern themselves by rules of almost incredible strictness and complexity.

**English delusions.** Half a century ago English people interested in India commonly cherished the belief that caste was destined to disappear within a measurable period, as the result of secular education combined with missionary effort. For instance, the able author of the Le Bas prize essay, published in 1853, ventured to prophesy:

> 'It will die away by degrees, as the people become better educated and more enlightened. The institution of schools on a liberal plan for the benefit of the rising generation in the *upper*, as well as the lower ranks of life, will do more probably to removing the prejudices of the natives, in regard to caste and religion, than direct attempts at conversion.'

The perilous delusion that the multiplication of schools, colleges, or other European institutions will lead to the withering or extinction of caste still survives, and unfortunately disfigures the Report. That delusion underlies the whole of paragraph 149 already cited, which treats of 'the duty of the educated classes to the ryots' in terms not to be reconciled with notorious facts. It crops up again in paragraph 152, where the authors gravely suggest that representative institutions in India 'will help to soften the rigidity of the caste system'. They are even sanguine enough to 'hope that those incidents of it which lead to the permanent degradation and ostracism of the lowest castes will tend to disappear in proportion to the acceptance of the ideas on which the new constitution rests'. The stupendous rashness of such phrases, which might be merely startling in a magazine article, becomes highly dangerous when the phrases are put forth by the Secretary of State and the Governor-General as justification for their policy and as part of the foundation for an Act of Parliament. Can the authors of the Report seriously believe that the multiplication of elections and ballot-boxes can affect the relative position of the Brahman and the low-caste man? If they do believe that they can believe anything. Have they observed that the active working of the elective system in the Calcutta and Bombay Corporations has softened the rigidity of the rules of caste in those cities? Certainly nobody else has noted such a phenomenon or dreamt of any connexion between the two things.

**Origin of the illusion.** The illusion that the caste institution is destined to weaken or disappear within a comparatively short period seems to rest chiefly upon a vague unreasoning faith that things wished for must happen. So far as it has any basis of fact the hypothesis seems to have been suggested partly by the well-known laxity in certain respects of the few Hindus who visit Europe or America, and partly by observation of the more general relaxation of certain rules or practices for the sake of convenience. For example, the necessities of cheap railway travelling compel people to crowd into carriages and touch one another closely for many hours, regardless of scruples dating from times when railways were not thought of. Similarly, the immense practical advantages of a copious supply of good water from stand-pipes in the larger towns are permitted to outweigh the ceremonial pollution which undoubtedly takes place. Ingenious pundits are not slow to find texts or to invent legal fictions in order to justify the deviation from ancestral custom. Many other cases of a like kind might be cited, as may be read in Ketkar's book.

**Superficial modifications.** But such merely superficial modifications of caste regulations dictated by imperative reasons of convenience do not touch the essence of the institution or weaken in the slightest degree the innate, inherited sentiment of caste exclusiveness. The Brahman who rides in a third-class carriage or drinks pipe-water does not think any better of his low-caste neighbour than when he travelled on foot and drank from a dirty well. The caste sentiment, so far from weakening, grows stronger in the higher castes, because caste and Hinduism are not two things but one thing, indivisible, and the revival of Hinduism in modified forms during recent years is notorious. A Hindu revival carries with it the stimulation of the caste sentiment essential to Hinduism.

**Caste will endure.** The foregoing discussion leads inevitably to the conclusion that prophecies or hopes of the weakening or disappearance of caste within a measurable period are futile. So long as Hindus continue to be Hindus, caste cannot be destroyed or even materially modified.

The deep waters of Hinduism are not easily stirred, and ripples on the surface leave the depths unmoved. The caste institution has lasted for three thousand years or more because it suits Hindus and has become part of their nature. For the same reason in all probability it will still endure for untold centuries. Nevertheless, it is difficult to contradict the saying of Mr. Archer that 'caste is a vice which affects India, all India, and in its extreme development, nothing but India. Its tyranny will have to be broken before India can become a nation among other modern nations.' Reformers must, I am convinced, make the best they can for many generations of an extremely inconvenient antique institution which accords ill with modern conditions, and is avowedly irreconcilable with the ideas of equality and fraternity. The Hindu scriptures beyond question exalt the Brahman as 'the lord of all classes', and denounce all notions of the brotherhood of man, or equality before the law. The Brahman will continue to spurn the low-caste man, who will continue to submit and to regard the Brahman as a god.

**Caste and patriotism.** The reality of the obstacle presented by such facts to the development of a tolerably homogeneous Indian nation, not to speak of a modern democracy, needs no further exposition. The saying of a French author that a Hindu 'n'a pas d'autre patrie que la caste'—if it goes a little beyond the truth—is not far from it. Another French writer observes that 'the caste system permits the juxtaposition of political and social elements, but does not produce their fusion; they mingle, but they do not combine'. Sir Harry Stephen affirms correctly that 'the whole idea of politics apart from religion is foreign to India; religion comes first and pervades everything, and in all social relations finds expression in the laws of caste'.

**Caste and law.** In March, 1858, when Sir Colin Campbell finally recovered Lucknow, he found sundry rebel proclamations, one of which expresses in admirably distinct language the essential opposition between the British policy of guaranteeing the equality of all men before the law, and the Indian doctrine that inequality, being of divine appointment, should be recognized by law and accepted as a governing principle determining the procedure and decisions of courts. The proclamation states accurately the practice of the indigenous governments, which was in accordance with the rules of the Hindu law books. The words were:

> 'All the Hindoos and Mohammedans know that man loves four things most: (1) his religion and caste; (2) his honour; (3) his own and his kinsmen's lives; (4) his property. All these four are well protected under native rulers; no one interferes with any one's religion; every one enjoys his respectability according to his caste and wealth. All the respectable people—Syed, Shaikh, Mogul, and Patan, among Mohammedans; and Brahmins, Chatrees, Bys, and Kaeths, among the Hindus—are respected according to their castes. No low-caste people like chamars, dhanook, and passees [*scil.* leather-dressers, village watchmen, etc.] can be equal to and address them disrespectfully. No one's life or property is taken unless for some heinous crime.
>
> 'The British are quite against these four things—they want to spoil every one's caste, and wish both the Mohammedans and Hindoos to become Christians. Thousands have turned renegades, and many will become so yet; both the nobles and low caste are equal in their eyes; they disgrace the nobles in the presence of the ignoble; they arrest or summon to their courts the gentry, nawabs, and rajahs at the instance of a chamar, and disgrace them.'

The document expresses faithfully the present-day sentiments of all high-caste Indians, not excluding those who now pose as democrats. It also emphasizes vividly the extent to which Indian Muhammadanism has been corrupted by the Hindu caste spirit.

**Brahmans.** The most essential feature of the caste organization is the high rank claimed by and generally conceded to the Brahmans, who number about ten millions.

The ancient author of the *Institutes of Manu,* whose authority is recognized all over India, lays down the propositions that

'A Brahman, whether learned or unlearned, is a mighty divinity' (ix. 317).

'By his origin alone a Brahman is a deity, even for the gods' (xi. 85).

'The Brahman is the lord of all classes' (x. 3).

A saying or syllogism, which has 'gained universal currency in India', emphasizes and justifies those propositions:

'The whole world is under the power of the gods,
The gods are under the power of the *mantras* (magic formulae),
The *mantras* are under the power of the Brahman;
The Brahman is therefore our God' (J. Wilson, i. 25).

We need not be surprised that men who are believed by themselves and others to be superior even to the gods should display arrogance towards the members of other castes, and regard the 'outcaste castes' as hardly human. Brahman arrogance is much more marked in the South than in the North and there leads to extreme oppression of the 'untouchable' classes, who are, for instance, hindered in the free use of the public roads lest their shadow should pollute a passing Brahman. Even now the Cheruma cultivators in Malabar have to assert their right to use the highways, which was denied them under Hindu rule.

In the Travancore State a Pulayan was, and probably still is, forbidden to enter a village. The regulations required that a Sūdra, or common Hindu, should not approach a Nāmbudri Brahman nearer than three feet. The distance to be kept by an outcaste might be as much as twenty or thirty paces. The exact regulations varied in different localities, but the spirit of all was one. Under the British government the extremities of Brahman oppression have to be restrained, because the law makes no distinction of persons. The last considerable Brahman government in India, that of the Peshwas, was extremely harsh both to the outcastes and to the wild tribes like the Bhīls.

**'Untouchables.'** It is no wonder that the eighteen millions of 'untouchables' in the Madras Presidency alone should seek to escape from their intolerable position by frequently embracing Christianity in large numbers at a time. Similar 'mass movements' occur in the Punjāb, and a like attraction is exercised by Islam in Eastern Bengal. The addresses presented to Mr. Montagu offer abundant evidence of the terror felt by the non-Brahman classes at the prospect of the Brahman domination opened up by the suggested constitutional changes. History justifies their fears.

**Minorities and majorities.** In the countries of Western Europe protection against the tyranny not infrequently practised by democracies is required by minorities. Ingenious politicians seek to provide the required protection by elaborate devices for proportional representation and so forth.

Such devices are difficult to work and notoriously ineffective. The saying that 'minorities must suffer' has abundant justification in the facts of constitutional history.

In India, as the authors of the Report unwillingly acknowledge (e.g. in para. 155 and elsewhere), huge *majorities* require protection against the arrogance of a small high-caste and chiefly Brahman minority supported, as is believed, by divine sanction.

The facts are incontrovertible and merit far more prominence than they have received in the Report. It cannot be too often repeated that sonorous phrases and the conventional language of parliamentary democracy cannot alter the facts, nor will copy-book maxims restrain the passions of mankind.

**Caste animosity.** The government finds it nearly as difficult to preserve the peace between the castes as between the creeds. In the South, especially, where the castes are more distinctly tribal than they are in the North, the animosity between different castes reaches an almost incredible height. It never dies out, and a feud, begun perhaps a thousand or two thousand years ago, is still as hot as ever. A curious and unexplained division of the non-Brahman castes into 'right-hand' and 'left-hand' groups is peculiar to the Peninsula, and is known to have existed in the eleventh century of the Christian era. Probably it is many ages older than that. The animosity between the two sets of castes never wanes and is frequently raised to boiling point by incidents which appear to other people to be absolutely trivial and insignificant. Such trifles suffice to provoke violent affrays and to harass the police of the Madras Presidency with never-ceasing anxiety. An astonishing example of an ancient feud surviving to the present day is recorded by the Madras Epigraphist, a Hindu scholar, in his Report for 1916–17. An inscription in the Tinnevelly district dating from A.D. 1452, and referring to a document nearly a century older, records the decree of the Vellāla caste concerning the penalties to be inflicted on the members of a lower caste, the Vellai-Nādār, who had given offence. The decree of the assembly provided for the immediate execution of three persons, and the killing of twenty-three others wherever they might be found. No member of the Vellai-Nādār community was to be allowed to enter a Tamil district, and many other stringent disabilities were imposed. The learned Epigraphist comments that 'the natural [*scil.* innate] hatred which the Vallālars of the present day still entertain for the Nādārs or Shānārs in the Tinnevelly district could possibly receive some explanation in the light of the facts of this curious record'. The lapse of seven centuries has not been enough to heal a feud which even at the time of the battle of Crécy probably was of immemorial antiquity. Yet the idealists are sanguine enough to think that futile wishes, solemn admonitions, and contested elections will do in a few years what seven centuries have failed to effect. *O sancta simplicitas!*

**Summary.** The inquiry has established the propositions that the institution of caste is at least three thousand years old; that it is universally believed to be of divine origin; that it concerns 250 millions of people, more or less; that it involves the division of the whole Hindu population and a large part of the Muslim and Christian minority into about 3,000 distinct hereditary castes, without reckoning sub-castes; that no Hindu can escape from the dominion of caste; that Hinduism and caste being one and indivisible, the institution cannot be abolished, and will still last for centuries; that the supremacy of the Brahman will continue to be acknowledged; that superficial modifications in the details of practice do not affect the caste spirit, which has been strengthened by the Hindu revival; that the doctrine of the equality of all men before the law is opposed to the Hindu scriptures and the practice of Hindu governments; that caste animosities, which are most bitter in the South, dating back for a thousand years or more, are as virulent as ever at this day; and that, consequently, peace and order require for their preservation a strong and impartial executive.

Those propositions state conditions which underlie all projects of constitutional reform, and for that reason deserve the earnest attention of reformers and of Parliament. No legislation can change them, and their gradual automatic relaxation must be deferred to a time so distant as to be beyond the vision of practical politics.

# CHAPTER 5

## 'VAIN VISIONS'

**Forebodings.** The sanguine prophecies in which the authors of the Report so freely indulge recall the 'vain visions' beheld by the misguided soothsayers of Israel who daubed with untempered mortar the wall that they had built. Should the building of the new Indian constitution be proceeded with solely on the lines of the Report, it is difficult to avoid forebodings that the wall built with the untempered mortar of English parliamentarism may suffer the fate predicted by Ezekiel and be 'brought down to the ground so that the foundation thereof shall be discovered', dragging with it in its fall the builders 'consumed in the midst thereof'.

If it be true that the visions guiding the plans of the Secretary of State and his colleague are in the nature of a dream or mirage, the structure erected under such guidance must needs be insecure. While the details of the machinery of government may be varied freely without incurring serious risk, a complex mechanism constructed on erroneous principles necessarily breaks down. When the constructive plan is sound, the pattern of the wheels and springs is susceptible of endless modification, but no skill in the manufacture of individual parts can compensate for error in the design of the mechanism as a whole. The authors of the Report, who display an uncanny ingenuity in elaborating the racks and pinions of their clockwork, are not equally successful in providing the motive power needed to make the clock go. Careful examination of the passages in the

Report which disclose the hopes and intentions of its authors is much more profitable than minute criticism on their ingenious concrete proposals, which are certain to be largely modified.

**'The basis of the whole system.'** Some such passages are so astonishing that they invite the denunciation heaped upon them by certain critics. But it is better to refrain from strong language and to allow the extracts to speak for themselves, with the minimum of comment.

Paragraph 131, dealing with 'the basis of a system of responsibility', states that 'the system [*scil.* of responsible government in the English parliamentary sense] presupposes in those who work it such a perception of, and loyalty to, the common interests as enables the decision of the majority to be peaceably accepted. This means that majorities must practise toleration and minorities patience.

'There must, in fact, be, not merely a certain capacity for business. but, what is much more important, a real perception of the public welfare as something apart from, and with superior claims to, the individual good. The basis of the whole system is a lively and effective sense of the sanctity of other people's rights.'

The dry comment of Dr. T. M. Nair that 'in India we have not got as far as that yet' might be developed and illustrated to an indefinite extent. Readers of Chapters 3 and 4 in this book will find many reasons for regarding the ideal of the authors of the Report as a 'vain vision'. Suppose that the 'basis' gives way, will not the 'whole system' fall like the wall daubed with untempered mortar?

**'The faith.'** The principles enunciated in paragraph 144 devoted to the 'justification of an advance' are still more startling than the ill-founded expectations noticed above. The authors assert that 'the placid, pathetic contentment of the masses is not the soil' on which to grow the plant of 'Indian nationhood'. Inasmuch as 'the faith that is in' them rests on the dogma that such 'nationhood within the Empire represents something better than anything India has ever attained', they believe that in 'deliberately disturbing' the contentment of the masses they are 'working for her highest good'.

The authors, when writing in that fashion, follow the lead given by their mentor, Mr. Curtis, who boldly declares that 'you must have the nerve to see Indian electorates hurt others—the helpless as well as themselves. It is the only way in which the spirit of trusteeship can be called into being and made to grow.' He, like his official pupils, cherishes 'the hope that the people of India may have learned such trust in each other that minorities will not insist' on protecting themselves by machinery designed to limit the power of the majority. Mr. Curtis maintains that 'only by suffering a people will learn the faculty of self-help and a genuine electorate be brought into being'.

It is difficult to comment with restraint on such dangerous doctrine. Supposing it to be true that the Indian masses generally are contented, why is such contentment 'pathetic'? Contentment, so far as it exists, is to be deliberately disturbed by the rulers of India in order to promote the ideal of Indian nationhood, the formation of a genuine electorate, and the development of the faculty of self-help. Do the high officials charged with the government of India, who propose deliberately to disturb the contentment of three hundred millions of Asiatic people, mostly ignorant, superstitious, fanatical, and intensely suspicious, realize what they are doing? Have they counted the cost? Once the disturbance of content has been fairly started among the untutored masses, no man can tell how far the fire may spread. Discontent will not be directed to the political objects so dear to Mr. Montagu and Mr. Curtis. It will be turned fiercely upon the casteless, impure foreigner, and, inflamed by the cry of 'religion in danger', will attract every disorderly element and renew the horrors of 1857 or the great anarchy of the eighteenth century. The lesson of history cannot be mistaken. Serious disturbance of contentment in India results invariably in an outburst of religious fanaticism. Any excuse, a house-tax, a canal rate, a sanitary regulation, is good enough to serve as the match to the conflagration. The Prime Minister's ideal of 'a happy, a prosperous, and a contented people' is the true one for India as for England.

Is it a light thing to promise 'suffering' as the first-fruits of political reform? The sufferers will turn and try to rend the government, to which they will ascribe their pain. 'God help a government of educated Indians', as Sir John Hewett remarks, 'when the people come to realize that they are being badly governed by it.' If, in order to obtain the blessings of contested elections, we must have the nerve to watch the helpless being hurt by the strong, is it not possible that the blessing may be bought at too high a price? Is the prospect of oppression and disorder thus held out likely to win the approval of sane, practical members of Parliament? It is legitimate for the critic to combine the outspoken cynicism of the utterances of Mr. Curtis with the more plausible phrases of the authors of the Report, because the propositions stated so nakedly by the amateur constitution-maker are implied in the principles enunciated by his official pupils.

**The ryot.** The long paragraph dealing with the 'political education of the ryot' is so manifestly opposed to all experience and so remote from realities that it is best refuted by reprinting it.

**Political education of the ryot.**

146. Let us begin with the ryot, because his is the most difficult case. When local bodies are developed some of his class will have a vote on local questions. He will thus begin to discover that if there is no school near his village or no road to take him to market, the right way

to procure these benefits is, not as heretofore by asking the Collector for them, but by voting for the local board member who is most likely to get them for him. The process will be an up-hill one; it will take time; and very probably advance can only come through previous failure. The rural voter will perhaps find himself cajoled or bought or coerced into voting in a way that does himself no good. But eventually it will dawn upon him, as it has done upon the agricultural classes elsewhere, that because he has a vote he has the means of protecting himself and that if those who claim to represent him neglect his interests he can discard them. As his political education proceeds he will come to apply the lesson learned in local affairs to the affairs of Government also. It will occur to him eventually that, if landlords are oppressive and usurers grasping and subordinate officials corrupt, he has at his command a better weapon than the *lathi* or the hatchet with which to redress his wrongs. He will gradually learn that though the Government is far off he can take a remote part in determining its action, and he will find that because the infinitesimal power which he wields is in the aggregate effective the Government becomes more sensitively alive and responsive to his needs. But his rate of progress will always depend upon the measure of assistance which he receives; and we look to both officials and candidates to feel a responsibility for helping him. Finally, he will come to realize that if he is to deal effectively with the more clever and better educated men who represent him in the councils he must acquire learning; and education, which he rejected so long as it merely seemed to him to clash with his material interests by depriving him of his children's labour and then unfitting them to follow the plough after him, will acquire in his eyes a new attractiveness when it presents itself to him as a factor in the process of getting better tenure or easier advances for himself. The present times are favourable to growth. The minds of India's peasant soldiery who have returned from abroad will never again work quite in the old way, and they will relate their experiences to many who stayed at home. But we feel no doubt that in learning to rise to his new responsibilities the Indian peasant voter will need all the help that other people, officials and non-officials alike, can give him.

Detailed criticism appears superfluous. It may suffice to say that not one of the prophecies has any chance of fulfilment.

**The landed aristocracy.** Paragraph 147, treating of the obligations of the landed aristocracy, also quoted in full, is equally contemptuous of notorious facts.

**Obligations of the landed aristocracy.**

147. The natural and acknowledged leaders in country areas are the landed aristocracy. They generally represent ancient and well-born families, and their estates are often the result of conquest or grants from some mediaeval monarch. By position, influence and education, they are fitted to take a leading part in public affairs. Some of them are beginning to do so; and our aim must be to call many more of them out into the political lists. They are conservative like the ryot, but like him they also will learn the need to move with changing times. They also, when they perceive that the protection of interests which are dear to them depends upon doing so, will find out how to organize, and to argue and to make speeches. It will be no very easy task for them. They stand upon a conception of social order which is not easily reconcilable with the hustings and the ballot-box. But undoubtedly they are called to take their place in the new régime, and to recognize that political life need not impair their dignity and self-respect. Like the representatives of their class in other countries they must learn to fulfil the responsibilities of their position in a new way. After all they start with considerable advantages, inasmuch as they have command both of means and position. We must give them a special measure of representation, if they need it, at the outset; but it may be that their political education, like the ryot's, will come mainly by pressure of events.

How can Mr. Montagu and Lord Chelmsford know that the Rajas and Nawabs *will* or *must* do the things demanded of them? Most assuredly they will *not* do anything of the kind. The sentence warning them that their political education has to come mainly by pressure of events seems to be a veiled threat of the 'suffering' predicted by Mr. Curtis.

**A precedent.** The idealism of the authors is nothing new. Similar fantastical expectations of what might be done by reformed landholders were formulated long ago in 1792-3 by Lord Cornwallis, and served as the basis of the policy on which the Permanent Settlement was founded. The Governor-General's sententious fatuities imposed even on ministers so able as Pitt and Dundas, who were ignorant of Indian conditions. The warning voice of Sir John Shore was unheeded and the zemindars of that day were ruined. Lord Cornwallis, who was ready to see them suffer, wrote:

'If there are men who will not follow this line of conduct when an opportunity is afforded them by the enaction of good laws, it surely is not inconsistent with justice, policy, or humanity to say that the sooner their bad management obliges them to part with their property to the more industrious, the better for the State.

'It is immaterial to Government what individual possesses the land, provided he cultivates it, protects the ryots, and pays the public revenue.'

Is it intended now that the 'pressure of events' should drive out the aristocrats who may decline to comply with the new 'good laws'?

Few persons free from personal interest in the business would deny that the Permanent Settlement legislation was a mistake. It certainly caused an enormous amount of ruin and misery for many years. In 1802 the Collector of Midnapore wrote that the new system

'has in the course of a very few years reduced most of the great zemindars of Bengal to distress and beggary, and produced a greater change in the landed property of Bengal than has, perhaps, ever happened in the same space of time, in any age or country by the mere effect of internal regulations'.

That extensive misery was caused by the unpractical

idealism of Lord Cornwallis, who asked from the landed aristocracy what it had not to give. His successors, who make on the landed aristocracy of to-day demands equally incapable of realization, are doomed to similar disappointment. The Rajas and Nawabs most assuredly will *not* 'find out how to organize, and to argue, and to make speeches'. They cannot change their nature any more than their predecessors could do so in the eighteenth century. So far as they are concerned the scheme will fail. How far they may be compelled to pay in 'suffering' for their inability to adopt English electioneering customs remains to be seen.

**'Our aim.'** The solemn warnings contained in paragraphs 150 and 151 cannot possibly be of the slightest use. Can any sane man believe that angry passions will be soothed by exhortations to contending factions that the cause of political progress

'ought to be dearer to them than their own sectional interests. So long as the latter are paramount any form of self-government to which India can attain must be limited and unreal at best. But our aim is that it should be complete and real, and to this end, as we have stated it, our reforms are designed.'

The aspirations of the authors are immaterial unless they lead to practical results. The question is how the reforms will work in this present imperfect world, not how they might work in an ideal world which never has existed or will exist.

Quotations of passages filled with platitudinous exhortation or impracticable idealism might be largely multiplied, but one more must suffice.

**The classes and the masses.** Innumerable petitions, addresses, pamphlets, and articles give forcible expression to the fears entertained by huge populations that reforms carried out on the lines of the Report may result in placing the majority of the people under the heel of a tyrannous Brahman oligarchy.

'We understand', certain memorialists argue, 'that our Rulers want our nation to be a self-supporting democracy; but we humbly submit that political liberty cannot prove a boon to a nation where the classes do not scruple to inflict the worst sort of injustice on those who are mostly ignorant and who, moreover, have been taught from times immemorial to bear it all as a matter of religious duty. And yet this is the real state of things in this country.'

The anxiety expressed in that extract and in many similar papers is fully justified by the facts of history and modern experience.

The reply of the authors of the Report is that they do not *intend* to create an oligarchy. As said before their intention does not matter, the question is what will be the practical effect of their proposals. Their words (paragraph 262, page 213) are:

'We regard the development of a broad franchise as the arch on which the edifice of self-government must be raised; for we have no intention that our reforms should result merely in the transfer of powers from a bureaucracy to an oligarchy.'

Thus the only security offered is a broad franchise. Little argument is needed to prove the inadequacy of that security in Indian conditions. Experience shows that the franchise will be used unwillingly and sparingly, that electioneering will fall chiefly into the hands of glib lawyers, and that the mass of voters will be as clay in the hands of the potter, if they can be induced to record their votes at all. We may apply the maxim of Bagehot that a very large constituency is 'the necessary, almost the legitimate, subject of electioneering management'. That is the experience everywhere. It offers but cold comfort to the non-Brahman memorialists.

Is it too much to expect that the readers of this chapter will agree that the authors of the Report are at times misled by 'vain visions' and in so far are unsafe guides?

# CHAPTER 6

## THE PROPOSALS OF THE REPORT AND SUGGESTIONS FROM OTHER SOURCES

**Five main heads of the Report.** The Report, as all students of it know to their cost, is long and contains much matter of various kinds. Its specific recommendations, however, may be condensed into a comparatively small space. They may be classified under five main heads, namely, those referring to (1) the Government of India, its constitution, and its relations with the Secretary of State and Parliament; (2) the Provincial Governments, with an elaborate scheme for dividing their jurisdiction between 'transferred' and 'reserved' subjects; (3) local self-government; (4) the public services, more especially the Indian Civil Service; and (5) franchise.

**Summary of head 1.** The lucid summary printed by Mr. Marriott, M.P., in the *Nineteenth Century* for September, 1918, gives the best short account of the recommendations under head 1, and I therefore take the liberty of reprinting it.

'1. *The Government of India.*

'The authors propose: (i) to give to the Imperial Parliament a more direct participation in Indian government by (*a*) putting the salary of the Secretary of State upon the Parliamentary Estimates; and (*b*) setting up at the beginning of each session a Select Committee of the House of Commons which shall present an annual report to the House on Indian affairs; (*c*) providing for a formal review, at stated intervals, of Indian policy; (ii) to keep the (Central) Government of India responsible to Parliament alone, but to reorganize the Government by (*a*) enlarging the Legislative Council to 100 members and giving it a majority of elected members; (*b*) setting up a Council of State or Second Chamber, half official, half non-official, which in matters certified as essential by the Government shall "have the last or the only word"; (*c*) instituting a Privy Council of India "as a means of honouring and employing ripe wisdom or meritorious service"; (*d*) giving greater elasticity "both in respect of size and distribution of work to the Governor-General's Executive Council and admitting thereto a Second Indian member", and finally (*e*) instituting a Council of Princes as a permanent consultative body, which should be invited to appoint annually a small Standing Committee to which the Viceroy might refer any difficulties affecting the Native States.'

2. *Provincial Governments.*

**Summary of head 2.** For exhibiting the proposed complicated constitution of Provincial Governments, it is convenient to utilize the official summary appended to the Report, omitting certain minor clauses for the sake of brevity.

THE PROVINCES.

Para. 189 23. The Provincial Governments to be given the widest independence from superior control in legislative, administrative, and financial matters which is compatible with the due discharge of their own responsibilities by the Government of India.

215, 218, 219, 238, 260 24. Responsible government in the provinces to be attained first by the devolution of responsibility in certain subjects called hereafter the transferred subjects (all other subjects being called reserved subjects), and then by gradually increasing this devolution by successive stages until complete responsibility is reached.

*Provincial Executives.*

214, 218, 220 25. The Executive Government in a province to consist of a Governor and Executive Council, a Minister or Ministers nominated by the Governor from the elected members of the Legislative Council, and an additional Member or Members without portfolios.

26. The Executive Council to consist of two Members, one of whom will be an Indian. Para. 218

Reserved subjects to be in the charge of the Governor and the Members of the Executive Council. 218

27. The Minister or Ministers to be appointed for the term of the Legislative Council, and to have charge of the transferred subjects. 218, 219

28. The additional Member or Members to be appointed by the Governor from among his senior officials for purposes of consultation and advice only. 220

29. The Government thus constituted to deliberate generally as a whole, but the Governor to have power to summon either part of his Government to deliberate with him separately. Decisions on reserved subjects and on the supply for them in the provincial budget to rest with the Governor and his Executive Council: decisions on transferred subjects and the supply for them with the Governor and the Ministers. 219, 221

*Provincial Legislatures.*

31. In each province an enlarged Legislative Council with a substantial elected majority to be established. The Council to consist of (1) members elected on as broad a franchise as possible, (2) nominated including (*a*) official and (*b*) non-official members, (3) ex-officio members. The franchise and the composition of the Legislative Council to be determined by regulations to be made on the advice of the Committee described in paragraph 53 by the Governor-General in Council, with the sanction of the Secretary of State, and laid before Parliament. 225, 232, 233

32. The Governor to be President of the Legislative Council with power to appoint a Vice-President. 236

Para. 254 33. The Governor to have power to dissolve the Legislative Council.

237 34. Resolutions (except on the budget) to have effect only as recommendations.

233 35. Nominated official members to have freedom of speech and vote except when Government otherwise directs.

252 39. Legislation on all subjects normally to be passed in the Legislative Council. Exceptional procedure is provided in the succeeding paragraphs.

252 40. The Governor to have power to certify that a bill dealing with reserved subjects is essential either for the discharge of his responsibility for the peace or tranquillity of the province or of any part thereof, or for the discharge of his responsibility for reserved subjects. The bill will then, with this certificate, be published in the Gazette. It will be introduced and read in the Legislative Council, and, after discussion on its general principles, will be referred to a grand committee; but the Legislative Council may require the Governor to refer to the Government of India, whose decision shall be final, the question whether he has rightly decided that the bill which he has certified was concerned with a reserved subject.

The Governor not to certify a bill if he is of opinion that the question of the enactment of the legislation may safely be left to the Legislative Council.

252 41. The grand committee (the composition of which may vary according to the subject-matter of the bill) to comprise from 40 to 50 per cent. of the Legislative Council. The members to be chosen partly by election by ballot, partly by nomination. The Governor to have power to nominate a bare majority (in addition to himself), but not more than two-thirds of the nominated members to be officials.

253 42. The bill as passed in grand committee to be reported to the Legislative Council, which may again discuss it generally within such time limits

as may be laid down, but may not amend it except on the motion of a Member of the Executive Council or reject it. After such discussion the bill to pass automatically, but during such discussion the Legislative Council may record by resolution any objection felt to the principle or details, and any such resolution to be transmitted with the Act to the Governor-General and the Secretary of State.

43. Any Member of the Executive Council to have the right to challenge the whole or any part of a bill on its introduction, or any amendment when moved, on the ground that it trenches on the reserved field of legislation. The Governor to have the choice then either of allowing the bill to proceed in the Legislative Council, or of certifying the bill, clause, or amendment. If he certifies the bill, clause, or amendment the Governor may either decline to allow it to be discussed, or suggest to the Legislative Council an amended bill or clause, or at the request of the Legislative Council refer the bill to a Grand Committee. Para. 254

44. All provincial legislation to require the assent of the Governor and the Governor-General and to be subject to disallowance by His Majesty. 254

45. The veto of the Governor to include power of return for amendment. 254

46. The Governor-General to have power to reserve provincial Acts. 254

*Finance.*

47. A complete separation to be made between Indian and provincial heads of revenue. 200, 201

48. Provincial contributions to the Government of India to be the first charge on provincial revenues. 206 & 256

49. Provincial Governments to have certain powers of taxation and of borrowing. 210, 211

50. The budget to be laid before the Legislative Council. If the Legislative Council refuses to accept the budget proposals for reserved subjects 256

the Governor in Council to have power to restore the whole or any part of the original allotment, on the Governor's certifying that, for reasons to be stated, such restoration is in his opinion essential either to the peace or tranquillity of the province or any part thereof, or to the discharge of his responsibility for reserved subjects. Except in so far as he exercises this power, the budget to be altered so as to give effect to resolutions of the Legislative Council.

*Modification of Provincial Constitutions.*

Para. 260 52. Five years after the first meeting of the new Councils the Government of India to consider any applications addressed to it by a provincial Government or a provincial Legislative Council for the modification of the list of reserved and transferred subjects. In such cases the Government of India with the sanction of the Secretary of State to have power to transfer any reserved subject, or in case of serious maladministration to remove to the reserved list any subjects already transferred and to have power also to order that the salary of the Ministers shall be specifically voted each year by the Legislative Council. The Legislative Council to have the right of deciding at the same or any subsequent time by resolution that such salary be specifically voted yearly.

3. *Local Self-government.*

**Summary of head 3.** The authors of the Report have not much to say concerning local self-government in areas smaller than a province, that is to say, in divisions, districts, cities, towns, and rural circles.

They give at the close of paragraph 188 their 'first formula', which is: 'There should be, as far as possible, complete popular control in local bodies, and the largest possible independence for them of outside control.'

That proposition is developed by some remarks in

paragraphs 192–197, with an intimation that the subject is under the consideration of the governments in India.

4. *The Public Services, especially the Civil Service of India, commonly called the Indian Civil Service.*

**Summary of head 4.** The thorny subject of the services is dealt with, not very comprehensively or satisfactorily, in paragraphs 313–327. The official summary is as follows:

64. Any racial bars that still exist in regulations or appointments to the public services to be abolished. Para. 315

65. In addition to recruitment in England, where such exists, a system of appointment to all the public services to be established in India. 316

66. Percentages of recruitment in India, with definite rate of increase, to be fixed for all these services. 316, 317

67. In the Indian Civil Service the percentage to be 33 per cent. of the superior posts, increasing annually by $1\frac{1}{2}$ per cent. until the position is reviewed by the Commission (paragraph 56). 317

68. Rates of pay to be reconsidered with reference to the rise in the cost of living and the need for maintaining the standard of recruitment. Incremental time-scales to be introduced generally and increments to continue until the superior grade is attained. The maximum of ordinary pension to be raised to Rs. 6,000 payable at the rate of 1*s*. 9*d*. to the rupee, with special pensions for certain high appointments. Indian Civil Service annuities to be made non-contributory, but contributions to continue to be funded. Leave rules to be reconsidered with a view to greater elasticity, reduction of excessive amounts of leave admissible, and concession of reduced leave on full pay. The accumulation of privilege leave up to four months to be considered. 318–321

69. A rate of pay based on recruitment in India to be fixed for all public services, but a suitable 322

allowance to be granted to persons recruited in Europe or on account of qualifications obtained in Europe, and the converse principle to be applied to Indians employed in Europe.

It does not seem necessary to give a formal summary of the remarks of the Secretary of State and the Viceroy concerning the Native or Protected States, commissions in the army, and certain other matters touched on in the Report.

Various suggestions from other sources will now be collected.

**Head 5.** It will be convenient to treat the fifth subject, the franchise, in connexion with those suggestions. The authors of the Report have not much to say on the matter, which has been handed over to a committee operating in India. The Report remains incomplete pending the result of the investigations of that committee.

**Proposal of a Royal Viceroy.** The Aga Khan (p. 77, &c.) would have the Viceroy when practicable the son or brother of the Sovereign, holding office on a non-political tenure. His Prime Minister should be appointed for the same term of office, about five years, and 'the Viceroy and Prime Minister would choose their British and Indian colleagues of the Cabinet'. The business of the Empire would be for the most part conducted by the Prime Minister and his colleagues, so that the Viceroy would be free to make extended tours, to 'set the tone of Indian and not merely high official society, and to generally encourage the development of social life in the provinces'. He should be the patron of the arts, and the source of all honours.

Mr. Vyasa Rao (pp. 75–85, 352) agrees that the Viceroy, as the direct representative of the Sovereign, should be a prince of the blood royal, and that he should be in immediate contact with the ruling princes of India. But, instead of entrusting the administration to a Prime Minister,

Mr. Vyasa Rao would prefer to place it in the hands of a Governor-General, taking precedence after the Viceroy, and so to preserve the ancient statutory office of Governor-General. He argues that the combination in one person of the two distinct offices of Viceroy and Governor-General is inexpedient.

**A Senate.** The Aga Khan looks forward to a federal constitution presided over by the Government of India, vested with powers of general control, and retaining in its own hands the army, navy, foreign relations, and certain other departments. After the establishment of a federal constitution, embracing the Protected States as well as British India, the small amount of centralized legislation necessary would be best effected by a Senate comprising representatives both of the States and the Provinces. 'The Government of India would be the connecting bond between great national provinces and principalities, united for common purposes, but varying in organic and natural unity, representing their diversified history, races, religions, and languages.' His Highness believes that India when thus federated would attract to itself the neighbouring nations and become the leading partner in an immense South Asiatic Federation.

**Reference to Secretary of State.** Mr. Vyasa Rao would retain the Imperial Legislative Council for British India, restricting the actual voting to non-official members, while the official members should be entitled to join in the debates, but not to vote. Thus the undignified spectacle of the official *bloc* voting to order would be avoided, and in the event of the non-official verdict being rejected by the Government of India the difference should be referred to the Secretary of State for final decision, or alternatively to a Board of Arbitration in London. In that way deadlocks due to conflict between the legislature and the executive would be obviated, and an official majority of votes need not be maintained.

**India Office.** All reformers, including Mr. Montagu and Lord Chelmsford, are agreed that the minute control now exercised by the India Office should be materially relaxed, and that the Government of India, however constituted, should be given greater freedom of action than it now enjoys. Such freedom is in no way dependent on the form of internal constitution adopted for the Government of India. The further suggestion is made by Mr. Vyasa Rao that the Council of the Secretary of State should be abolished and replaced by a small Committee of the India Office, entrusted with the business of the Office, except the patronage, which the Secretary of State should retain in his own hands. Mr. Vyasa Rao desires that the India Office should 'become, when the Council ceases to exist, an office of record and an agency for the transaction of business on behalf of the Secretary of State and the Government of India, maintained out of Indian revenues'. Any control necessary should be exercised by Parliament through the responsible minister, the Secretary of State, who should be 'unfettered by the shackles' of the Council, and free to exercise his discretion independently (p. 318).

**Provincial finance.** All parties seem to be agreed that the finance of the Provincial Governments should be disentangled from that of the Government of India. The financial proposals of the Secretary of State and Viceroy are contained in paragraphs 200–211 of the Report. Mr. Vyasa Rao proposes that each provincial administration should pay to the Supreme Government a fixed percentage of its income, so that each province may defray its upkeep and the development of its resources, while making a fair contribution for imperial purposes. The principle of the final separation of imperial from provincial finance being accepted, the details can be worked out by experts and in debate on the India Bill which must be introduced. Reformers of Indian birth are eager to secure the admission that the Government of India, however constituted, 'should be free to pursue in fiscal questions the policy most advantageous for the country'. No claim is more popular or pressed with greater insistence.

The necessities of Indian conditions plainly require the reservation by the Government of India of extensive executive powers to be exercised on due occasion. The Report (paragraph 289) frankly recognizes the fact that the Supreme Government must be provided with 'the machinery of autocracy' to be used in 'essential cases'.

His Highness the Aga Khan, who would entrust the control of finance and legislation, especially in the provinces, to elective assemblies, is convinced that 'a strong and independent executive' is required everywhere.

**Provincial governments.** All parties are agreed that the government of the major provinces should consist of a Governor and Executive Council, such council being appointed, if it does not already exist. While it is recognized that several of the existing provinces are inconveniently large for the efficient working of a government on lines more popular than at present, the Aga Khan is strongly opposed to a suggestion for breaking up the existing provinces into smaller units, based on race, language, and other national characteristics. He proposes in lieu of that arrangement certain adjustments of boundaries. He is opposed to the detachment of Burma from the Indian Empire, which is advocated by many people, including Mr. Curtis and the author of this book. Mr. Vyasa Rao would retain Burma as part of the Indian Empire, giving it Presidency rank, like Madras, Bombay, and Bengal.

The authors of the Report propose an arrangement under which the subjects within the jurisdiction of each provincial government shall be divided into two classes, 'transferred' and 'reserved'. The plan, sometimes described as 'diarchy', was borrowed from Mr. Curtis and has not found general favour with other reformers, or public opinion. In this place it is sufficient to say that the proposed machinery is excessively intricate and admittedly difficult to work.

The Aga Khan would be content with an enlarged elective assembly 'to control finance and legislation', and 'a strong independent executive, responsible to the Viceroy and Secretary of State for tenure of office and appointment'. If the elective assembly should reject a Government bill, he suggests that the bill simply should be dropped.

His idea that a ruling prince might be invited to leave his own territories and assume charge of a province in British India is not likely to be realized.

His Highness would like to see a Senate or second chamber of notables constituted for each province.

Mr. Vyasa Rao is of opinion that the governor or lieutenant-governor of a province ordinarily should not be a member of the Civil Service of India, 'the best available British and Indian talent' being utilized to fill the appointments, and that the Presidency form of government should be the model.

General agreement exists that the provinces should be much more autonomous than they now are, autonomy meaning freedom from the detailed administrative and financial control of the Government of India.

**Local self-government.** The Aga Khan, after noting the ill success in Russia of plans for working local self-government in connexion with a centralized bureaucracy, observes that

'happily the constant friction arising from the Russian experiment has not been reproduced in India, for the good and simple reason that the real power has never been out of the hands of the bureaucracy'.

He holds that the existence of an elective assembly at the head-quarters of the provincial government secures local co-operation, and that it is necessary that the application of popular control in the State should *precede* real local self-government in the smaller areas. Lord Crewe expressed the same idea in the House of Lords on October 24, 1918, when he doubted if the encouragement of local self-government should not 'begin at the top'.

'That', he said, 'was undoubtedly what we had done in this country. We started with something like a free and liberally elected Parliament in 1832, and it was not until two generations afterwards that we established county, district, and parish councils.'

The Aga Khan makes the practical suggestion that in order to give life to local self-government each province-state should be equipped with a ministry similar in function to the English Local Government Board, which, as Lord Ripon intended, 'should revise and check the acts of local bodies, but not dictate them'. That reasonable arrangement is very different from the unworkable 'diarchy' of the Report. His Highness believes that an elastic system could thus be built up, reaching down to the village *panchāyat* of elders.

Mr. Vyasa Rao approaches the problem from another point of view, and, in agreement with Lord Morley, would make 'the village a starting-point of public life'. While recognizing the truth that modern conditions make it 'well-nigh impossible' to restore the village organizations of ancient times, he believes that village autonomy can be revived, and all small causes and local matters left to the *panch* for disposal, without the intervention of lawyers. His proposal is not inconsistent with that of the Aga Khan, but he does not refer to the fact that nearly a century ago an attempt to restore *panchāyats* in the Madras Presidency was not a success, because the people did not care to use them.

**Public services.** We now turn to the more difficult and controversial subject of the Public Services, and more especially of the Civil Service of India, the *corps d'élite* now

(Government of India Act, 1915) called the Indian Civil Service, which at present has the largest share of the government in its hands, and is admitted to hold a most honourable record.

The recommendations in the Report cannot be said to grapple firmly with the problem. They deal chiefly with comparatively minor matters concerning pay, pension, and leave. The general remarks and sententious advice of the Secretary of State and the Viceroy will be found in paragraphs 323-327.

**Indian Civil Service.** Everybody seems to beagreed that it is desirable, if possible, to maintain for many years to come the specially trained Indian Civil Service as a body of experts, qualified by training and experience to undertake heavy responsibilities in the course of their career. Nobody seems to want at present to abolish the District Officer, otherwise called Magistrate and Collector, or Deputy Commissioner, who is the mainstay of the administration. Mr. Vyasa Rao would like to see him aided by an advisory District Assembly, meeting twice a year, and chiefly devoted to the ventilation of local grievances. It is evident that the changed conditions contemplated by reformers may make the career of an Indian Civil Servant so unattractive that it may be impossible to induce men of the requisite character and ability to join the Service. The authors of the Report see that danger, and endeavour to avert it by their proposals above mentioned. But they touch only lightly on the real difficulties, which go deeper than questions of pay, pension, and leave.

**Project of a training college.** Mr. Archer treats the subject with more insight in the 'postscript-proem' (dated May, 1917) prefixed to his book, *India and the Future*. He sees the truth that the object should be to catch the young men who feel a call to India, and not merely those who go solely for the sake of the material prospects offered. He advocates the establishment of a reformed Haileybury College, where all youths destined for the Indian Services generally would be trained together, without distinction of race or colour; where all the students would feel themselves dedicated to the service of India, and would be trained 'in a place where India should always be present, predominant, enthroned'. I have held the same opinion for many years past and am glad to learn that it has the powerful support of Lord Sydenham of Combe.

Sir John Hewett draws a gloomy picture of the effect of the 'reforms' on the services, and gives good reason for believing that the Indian Civil Service, in particular, has been 'going down the hill', at least since 1908. The condition of the Indian Medical Service also is far from satisfactory.

**Sec. 87 of Charter Act of 1833.** In all discussions of Service questions it is of the highest importance to bear in mind constantly the binding provisions of section 87 of the Charter Act of 1833, which runs:

> 'No native of the said territories nor any natural-born subject of His Majesty resident therein shall by reason of his religion, place of birth, descent, colour, or any of them, be disabled from holding any place, office, or employment under the Company.'

That comprehensive statutory enactment is still in force and cannot be affected by the action of any Secretary of State or Viceroy. Its provisions were emphasized by the Directors, who laid down the principle that 'no subject of the King, whether of Indian, British, or mixed descent, shall be excluded either from the posts usually conferred on our uncovenanted servants in India, or from the covenanted service itself, provided he be otherwise eligible, &c.' The terms apply equally to all persons domiciled or resident in India, whether Europeans or others. Any proposal to impose a statutory obligation that any particular office should be held by an 'Indian', in the sense of the old word 'native', is equivalent to the disqualification of Europeans in virtue of their 'religion, place of birth, descent, colour, or any of them'. The proposals made by the Public Services Commission and by the authors of the Report frequently offend against that canon, especially in requiring a fixed 'Indian' percentage in the Civil Service. Such proposals clearly introduce new racial distinctions in contravention of the Act and of the clear declaration by the authors of the Report (paragraph 315) that they would 'remove from the regulations the few remaining distinctions that are based on race, and would make appointments to all branches of the public service without racial discrimination'. They have failed to see that their recommendations over and over again introduce fresh racial discrimination in a novel form *as against Europeans or persons of European descent.*

If, in future, as proposed by the Report, many first appointments now made in England are to be made in India, they must be open to all classes alike. Any formal rule excluding Europeans or Anglo-Indians (otherwise called Eurasians),[1] Jews, or any other class, infringes the Act of 1833, which 'Indians' in the narrower sense have been accustomed to regard as their Magna Carta. That principle is often disregarded by amateur reformers as well as by the authors of the Report. It is needless to give instances.

A sharp distinction must be drawn between customary practice and a formal rule purporting to have the effect of law. For instance, it may properly become an ordinary practice to appoint a certain proportion of 'Indians' to Executive Councils, always provided that they are 'qualified

[1] The use of the term 'Anglo-Indians' for 'Eurasians', commonly supposed to be a perverse innovation made by Lord Hardinge of Penshurst, is nearly a century old (Sir John Malcolm, *Pol. Hist. of India*, 1826, vol. ii, pp. 260–4).

by their education, ability, and integrity', as required by Queen Victoria's proclamation of 1858, but a formal rule that so many members *must* be 'Indians' imposes a racial qualification with the correlative racial disqualification, and consequently is *ultra vires* as being opposed to both the Act of 1833 and the proclamation of 1858. Those enactments require the preservation of freedom in the choice of fit persons without any racial bar. Mr. Vyasa Rao rightly urges the necessity of giving 'full and free' play to both the British and the 'Indian' elements in the Services.

**Various suggestions.** The Aga Khan's suggestion that non-official persons should be appointed occasionally as district officers does not seem to be practicable for various reasons. His proposal that Commissioners of Divisions, where they exist, may be abolished, would effect a small financial saving and deserves consideration.

The Madras Presidency manages to get on without such officers, but something may be said in defence of their retention in the other Presidencies. They were first appointed by Lord William Cavendish-Bentinck about 1830.

Mr. Vyasa Rao deduces two principles on which to base the reorganization of the Services, namely (1) the absolute and entire abolition of all racial disability, which has been dealt with sufficiently, and (2) 'the fashioning of the services in regard to pay, prospects, and pension so as to meet the actual needs of the country, and not so as to furnish a selection of offices and openings for men of British birth'. That principle, also, may be accepted as sound. The difficulty lies in the application and the ascertainment of 'the needs of the country', so long as a considerable British element is necessary.

The same author works out a scheme for reorganization, but I do not propose to go into details, which require examination by a competent committee. When an Indain

Bill comes to be drafted, the difficult problem will have to be faced and solved somehow. The solution certainly will not coincide exactly with any of the tentative schemes proposed by individuals. It may be that in course of time the Indian Civil Service, notwithstanding its glorious record, may become superfluous, but that time is not yet.

### 5. *Franchise.*

**Franchise.** Questions relating to the franchise cannot be treated in any detail with advantage until the Commissions at work in India shall have reported, but even now certain large issues may be considered.

**Female franchise.** The Aga Khan maintains, with his accustomed boldness, that 'no scheme of political reform based on the co-operation of the people with the rulers can or will succeed, if it is vitiated by the radical defect of closing the door to women on the irrational ground of sex, and not accepting equal qualifications as conferring equal rights'.

Inasmuch as the franchise in India must necessarily be restricted in many ways, he sees no difficulty in the admission of women. The suggestion does not appear to have been made by anybody else, and few people are likely to accept the proposal of His Highness.

**Representation of interests.** General agreement exists that the conditions of India preclude the universal demarcation of purely territorial areas for constituencies as the basis of the franchise. While we may be permitted sometimes to feel doubts about the suitability of elective representation in India at all, elections by small constituencies to seats in Legislative Councils having been legalized since 1909, the assumption may be made that Parliament will sanction and require a considerable development of the use of elections.

Purely territorial demarcations of electoral areas being admittedly impracticable, the possible modifications of such areas are two only, namely (1) the representation of distinct 'interests', which Mr. Vyasa Rao terms 'institutional', and (2) the representation of communities, generally described as 'communal'. The representation of special interests, such as Chambers of Commerce, the mill industry, the talukdars of Oudh, &c., has been recognized in the Morley-Minto reforms, and seems destined to stay. That arrangement, in addition to its obvious convenience in India, has the historical advantage of being in accord with ancient English practice, as described by Bagehot (*English Const.*, 6th ed., p. 173), who states correctly that our ancestors

'laboured to give a *character* to the various constituencies, or to many of them. They wished that the shipping trade, the wool trade, the linen trade should each have their spokesman; that the unsectional Parliament should know what each section of the nation thought before it gave the national decision.'

It may be assumed that such sectional or 'institutional' representation will be continued in India as a practical necessity. Mr. Vyasa Rao, indeed, would give the principle a wide extension. He does not share the love of the authors of the Report for 'direct representation' of the individuals in each constituency, which he does not advocate at present. On the other hand, he holds it to be necessary that the representation of institutions and interests should be direct, without any filtration through Provincial Councils.

**'Communal' representation.** The subject of 'communal' representation is far more controversial, and the system undoubtedly is liable to weighty objections. Lord Morley unwillingly consented to give the Muhammadan community separate representation, a precedent now found to be extremely inconvenient. The Muhammadans will not surrender their privilege, so that Mr. Vyasa Rao's advice that it should be withdrawn or 'wiped out' cannot be adopted. In fact, the Secretary of State and the Viceroy propose to extend the privilege to the Sikhs, a much less easily defined community. It is extremely difficult to define a Sikh for electoral purposes. It is practically certain that but for the existence of the Sikh regiments with their strong *esprit de corps* the Sikhs before now would have been for the most part merged in Hinduism.

Where is communal representation to stop? Every creed, sect, and social section obviously cannot claim separate representation. The arguments against the system are stated forcibly by Mr. Vyasa Rao. On the other hand, the claim to such representation is pressed most insistently by many classes and communities, who fear the domination of Brahmans, lawyers, and so forth.

The Aga Khan strongly supports the claim to communal representation, which he would extend widely, so that each of the religions and races would 'provincially be a *millet*, to use the Turkish term, and each would have a fair share in the assembly directly elected'. He would allow special representation, for instance, to the huge mass of the non-Brahmans of Madras, whose contentions are upheld vigorously by the Indo-British Association. That body advocates the adoption of the 'communal principle' generally, so that all large communities, or groups of communities, may be represented by their own members. The principle is held to be essential in a caste-ridden country.

**The 'Spectator'.** The *Spectator*, while willing to accept the suggestions of the Association, would prefer to summon 'a purely native body', a sort of Indian National Convention, and ask that body to frame a plan, including specific suggestions for breaking down caste and providing adequate securities for minorities of various kinds. That plan is impossible, as will be apparent to anybody who takes the trouble to read carefully Chapter 4 in this book. The *Spectator* holds that 'nothing will be done of permanent value in the direction of Indian self-government till the caste system is got rid of, or so greatly modified as to be harmless. Such a change, it is argued, cannot be imposed from outside, and can be effected, if at all, only by the 'general assent of the majority of the Indian peoples'. That aspiration is a 'vain vision', because the required 'general assent' cannot forcibly be attained. Hindus, with few exceptions, do not wish to abolish caste, and cannot imagine themselves in a casteless condition.

**Various proposals.** The Indo-British Association and Lord Sydenham of Combe would seek to progress along the path of 'self-government' and to move towards 'the goal of responsible government', by the 'geographical method', explained as follows:

'In every province place one or two districts wholly under the Indian members of the different services. This has been done in Bengal, but the experiment is inconclusive because of the want of a revenue system. If, after a period of trial, this system is proved to work well, other districts can be similarly staffed. Later a Commissioner's division can be so handed over, and the process, if shown to be successful, can be continued until a whole province comes under Indian rule in the future.'

It seems unnecessary to discuss certain constitutional schemes worked out by Mr. Curtis and other people, which have been examined at length in the Report, and deservedly rejected.

The principal suggestions for reform made officially and otherwise having been reviewed, a few pages will be devoted to criticism, chiefly of the principles and proposals of the Report.

# CHAPTER 7

## CRITICISM

A CONSIDERABLE amount of criticism both on the Report and on suggestions from other quarters has been included in the earlier chapters of this book, but some remarks of a critical nature remain to be made, which possibly may prove helpful to the authorities with whom the final momentous decision must rest.

**Principle of the Report.** The most fundamental enunciation of principle in the Report is that expressed in paragraph 7 in the following words:

> 'The policy, so far as Western communities are concerned, is an old and tried one. Englishmen believe in responsible government as the best form of government that they know; and now in response to requests from India they have promised to extend it to India also under the conditions set out in the announcement. We need not dwell on the colossal nature of the enterprise, or on the immense issues of welfare or misery which hang upon its success or failure.'

That enunciation may be analysed into two propositions, namely (1) that a policy, assumed to have been successful in Western communities, *can* be applied to India; and (2) that such a policy *ought* to be applied to India, even at the request of an admittedly small body of Indians, because Englishmen believe it to be intrinsically the best.

The second proposition may be considered first. Few Englishmen either know or care much about India. The ignorance of the bulk of the new constituencies on the subject is abysmal, and the mere fact that voters steeped in ignorance may believe their own favourite institution to be suitable for a country concerning which they know practically nothing is no reason for forcing their crude prejudices upon a helpless dependency. It is the business of leaders to lead, and it is the plain duty of well-informed statesmen to guide their less instructed countrymen, who should not be left to follow blindly the dictates of their prepossession in favour of democratic formulae supposed to be of universal application. The prepossession undoubtedly exists and constitutes a grave danger in present conditions. It is indispensable that the democracy should be given guidance when dealing with subjects out of the range of its experience. The belief of the ordinary British voter that 'responsible government' is the best possible form of government for any country is in reality wholly irrelevant.

**The true issue.** The true issue is whether or not such government is for the good of India and also of England. We must assume that the close political connexion of the two countries will subsist for many years, and that consequently benefits or injuries done to India will react upon England. While proposals of reform must contemplate primarily the good of India, their reflex action upon England should not be overlooked. If 'responsible government' in the parliamentary sense be not really suitable for India and yet should be forced upon her by doctrinaire politicians, both India and England will feel the ill effects. If statesmen come to the conclusion that such government, whatever be its merits elsewhere, cannot be fitted to India, and they decline accordingly to force it upon that land, their decision will be readily accepted both by the rank and file of the members of parliament and by the constituencies, who will not hesitate to follow the guidance on a difficult and unfamiliar subject offered by trusted leaders.

It might not be difficult to make a strong case for the

contention that even in Western communities 'responsible government' has not been an invariable success, but there is no need to go into that question. Assuming 'responsible government' to be the best for Western Europe, *ought* it to be extended to India, which has little in common with European nations? If my readers have succeeded in grasping the statements of fact made in Chapters 2, 3, and 4 of this book they can hardly fail to realize the immensity of the gulf which separates India from Europe in matters political.

**A 'new structure'.** All parties are agreed that nothing like 'responsible government' now exists or ever has existed in India. It follows that the new constitution as proposed, aiming at and striving gradually to attain 'the goal of responsible government', must be an absolute breach of all tradition and continuity. It is a purely foreign invention exported from England. The authors of the Report frankly admit that it is so when they say (paragraph 101) that 'the old structure does not admit of development . . . we must, therefore, create a new structure'. That is 'a large order', if an expressive slang phrase may be excused. Obvious *prima facie* objections exist against tearing up by the roots old institutions in an Asiatic country inhabited by three hundred millions of people, and replanting the ground with a delicate 'new structure' imported ready made from Europe. The undertaking is bold, and may be described as rash, perhaps even as reckless. Certainly it is dangerous.

**Cautions.** Might it not be wiser to accept the principle enunciated by an ardent and radical reformer, and to be content with a scheme designed to give the least possible occasion for controversy by reason of sudden and abrupt breach with the past? Especially, if, as seems possible, such a scheme can be brought into operation quickly, the superior wisdom of the more cautious course appears to be self-evident.

The introduction of foreign political machinery seems to be hardly consistent with 'self-government', while action based upon abstract doctrines is notoriously apt to fail in practice. Prudence suggests the expediency of confining the inevitable changes to moderate adaptations of existing machinery.

The Report, as already noted, ignores the existence of the King-Emperor and makes no attempt to utilize the fervent Indian sentiment of loyalty to His Majesty's person, which, when rightly viewed, presents a golden link uniting the British democracy with the princes and peoples of India. Those reasons and many others which might be elaborated at wearisome length indicate that the fundamental principle of the Report needs searching examination.

We are thus led to consider the precise meaning of the terms 'self-government' and 'responsible government'.

**'Self-government.'** The premiss that India must remain 'within the Empire', and subject to parliamentary control for an indefinite number of years, although not necessarily for ever, rules out the meaning of 'independence' for the term 'self-government'.

No responsible politician, Indian or British, proposes that within any time now in sight the political connexion between India and England should be severed in such a way as to leave India absolutely alone with the obligation to defend herself by her own army and navy unaided, as well as to provide a complete civil government. That being clearly impossible, 'self-government' must mean something much less than complete national independence. A large measure of 'self-government' or 'autonomy' in a limited sense can be arranged any day by means of legislation or executive order, simply by relaxing the excessively minute control now exercised by the Secretary of State and the India Office. That kind of 'self-government' is absolutely independent of the internal form of the Government of

India, and could be granted if every member of that government was an Englishman, and if the powers of the government were autocratic in the strictest sense. All parties are agreed that the external control over the Government of India ought to be relaxed. But such relaxation would not satisfy the demand for 'self-government', which is understood to imply the government of India by Indians, so far as may be. The reformers of Indian birth ardently desire that a much larger proportion of the higher offices should be held by Indians than is now the case, and that general policy, especially in the fiscal domain, should be directed to meet Indian rather than British opinion.

The government and administration of India by born Indians is only partially attainable. It has been in process of gradual realization for a long time past, and public opinion, British and Indian, is in favour of the extension and quickening of the process within the limits imposed by essential conditions.

**Conditions.** One of those conditions is that the naval and military defence of India is an imperial concern and must remain so for a period beyond the ken of present-day politics. Another is that the main lines of policy must conform to the ideas of the British nation, a requirement which involves the retention of a substantial British element in the administration, especially in the higher grades. That limitation of 'self-government' is frankly acknowledged in the Report. A third necessity is that a reasonably high standard of good and progressive government must be maintained with regard to the interests of both India and England. The doctrine, favoured by the authors of the Report, that learners in the school of political evolution should be suffered to make mistakes and endure 'growing pains' involves grave dangers and must not be pushed too far.

**'Geographical method.'** The 'geographical method'

for the extension of 'self-government' (*ante*, p. 77), as advocated by Lord Sydenham of Combe, is unacceptable because it would accentuate racial animosities, as well as for other reasons.

**'Responsible government' in England.** The term 'responsible government' is more difficult, obscure, and controversial.

In modern English politics it means that the Executive Government, composed of members of both Houses of Parliament, is responsible to the House of Commons, and must go out of office when it loses the confidence of that House. Such loss of confidence is usually expressed by an adverse vote deliberately given on a subject which the Government decides to treat as a test question. The defeated Government is bound to resign. When the ministry of party *A* goes out, another ministry formed from party *B* comes in. The arrangement postulates the existence of rival organized parties. It further requires that all the principal members of the Executive Government should be also members of either House of Parliament, and that either of the organized parties should be prepared to supply a body of persons qualified to form a capable administration. That definition exactly describes the practice as before the war, but that deadly struggle has somewhat complicated the situation by the introduction of coalition governments and the suspension of ordinary party politics. The tendency, however, is towards the restoration of the party system as soon as peace is declared. In fact, British politicians do not know how to work any other system.

**Indian conditions.** It is obvious that similar conditions in India do not exist, never have existed, and are not likely to come into existence within any time that can be foreseen. Whether or not it is desirable that they should ever be brought into being in India is a purely speculative matter which need not be discussed. It is certain that 'the goal of responsible government' mentioned in the 'pronouncement' cannot mean for India exactly what it means to the ordinary member of Parliament.

Nobody in his senses can expect to live to see the time when the Imperial Legislative Council or Assembly at Delhi shall have expanded into a Parliament with organized parties, capable of supplying from its own members not only one complete ministry, but also an alternative one.

**Definition in the Report.** What then is the meaning of the phrase 'the goal of responsible government'?

It is not easy to say. It certainly cannot bear the ordinary parliamentary signification. The authors of the Report, eager to bring the phrase into their programme, have invented a new definition for Indian purposes. Their scheme of 'diarchy' for provincial governments provides that 'transferred subjects' shall be in charge of Indian-born ministers selected from the provincial legislative council or assembly, who should be appointed for the duration of that body, namely, three years, and be compelled to seek re-election after that time. For that reason they are described as being 'responsible to their constituents' (*ante*, p. 59). The definition will be found in paragraphs 189 and 215, as follows:

189. 'When we come to the provincial Governments the position is different. Our objective is the realization of responsible government. We understand this to mean, first, that the members of the executive government should be responsible to, because capable of being changed by, their constituents; and, secondly, that these constituents should exercise their power through the agency of their representatives in the assembly. These two conditions imply in their completeness that there exist constituencies based on a franchise broad enough to represent the interests of the general population, and capable of exercising an intelligent choice in the selection of their representatives; and, secondarily, that it is recognized as the constitutional practice that the executive Government retains office only so long as

it commands the support of a majority in the assembly. But in India these conditions are as yet wanting. . . . The considerations of which we took account in Chapter VI forbid us immediately to hand over complete responsibility. We must proceed therefore by transferring responsibility for certain functions of government while reserving control over others. From this starting-point we look for a steady approach to the transfer of complete responsibility. We may put our second formula thus:

'*The provinces are the domain in which the earlier steps towards the progressive realization of responsible government should be taken. Some measure of responsibility should be given at once, and our aim is to give complete responsibility as soon as conditions permit.* . . .

215. 'We start with the two postulates that complete responsibility for the government cannot be given immediately without inviting a breakdown, and that some responsibility must be given at once if our scheme is to have any value. We have defined responsibility as consisting primarily in amenability to constituents, and in the second place in amenability to an assembly. We do not believe that there is any way of satisfying these governing conditions other than by making a division of the functions of the provincial Government, between those which may be made over to popular control and those which for the present must remain in official hands.'

The object avowed is to drag in the formula 'responsible government' somehow, and the result is an unheard-of definition of the term. The 'responsibility to constituents' invented by the authors of the Report obviously is unreal, a mere piece of lip-service to a formula. When the almost universally condemned and wholly unworkable 'diarchy' is dropped, as it must be, 'responsibility to constituents' goes with it.

**Other opinions.** Little help is to be derived from Dr. T. M. Nair's attempt at a definition, which is: 'The Government is responsible to the representatives of the People, and not of small sections of it.'

When the Aga Khan was writing in 1917, after the

'pronouncement', but before the publication of the Report, he showed his consciousness of the inconveniences lurking in the phrase 'goal of responsible government'. The principal part of his observations is quoted in the extract on the fly-leaf. He has no difficulty in proving that 'responsible government' in the English parliamentary sense is a product of the party system and a purely insular piece of mechanism. Other nations, notably the United States of America, manage to make their executive governments responsible to the people by methods of a totally different kind. There is nothing so sacred in the peculiar English method as to make it universally applicable to countries where the conditions differ completely from those of Great Britain.

**An interpretation.** We thus arrive at the practical conclusion that Indian reformers need not be in a hurry to reach forward to the distant 'goal of responsible government', whatever be the meaning attached to that elusive catchword. They have plenty to do in trying to grasp the more solid object of 'self-government', to the utmost attainable extent, subject to the limitations explained above. The phrase 'responsible government', in so far as it can be applied practically to Indian institutions, must needs be used in a somewhat indefinite sense, as connoting a government sensitive to Indian public opinion expressed through elective assemblies and other channels. The circumstances of the present time are such that the Government of India is likely to feel its responsibility to Indian public opinion too much rather than too little. If it should ever display any signs of insensibility or irresponsibility, the control of Parliament, and especially the check exercised by the proposed sessional committee, will amply suffice to keep it up to the mark.

The somewhat tedious although indispensable discussion of definitions being thus ended, we pass to other topics.

**Periodical commissions.** If the Secretary of State and

the Viceroy be allowed to have their way, and frequent commissions of inquiry into the working of the revised constitution are to overhaul the constitutional machinery every few years, the unhappy Government of India will never have a moment's rest. It will be unable to feel any assurance as to the form which it will be made to assume, and it will be so busy trying to justify its existence that it will have little time for its proper work. Sir J. P. Hewett, who knows his subject from the inside, tells us that 'the real trouble about the Government of India is that for the last ten years or more it has ceased to attempt to govern', or, in other words, to fulfil the purpose for which it exists. What will it be like if it has to pretend to do its duty under the whip of nearly continuous commissions?

The resulting agitation and intrigues would be unceasing, while the paralysis of the executive would be all but complete. Yet India as a whole, and each Indian province or district, urgently needs a strong executive at all times. The lessons of history and experience to that effect are so plain to read as hardly to need detailed exposition. Some of the reasons why an executive swift and decisive in action is indispensable will be found in the earlier chapters of this essay.

**Council of State**. The Report proposes to secure the necessary support for the Government of India, if it should be confronted with a hostile Legislative Assembly, by means of needlessly complicated devices. The unedifying spectacle of the official majority in the Legislative Council, as now constituted, voting to order collectively as a *bloc* is rightly disliked. The authors of the Report propose to give up the official majority in the Imperial Legislative Council or Assembly, and to obtain compensation by the creation of a Senate or Council of State, which apparently should ordinarily have an official majority of one only, a rather narrow margin. Measures deemed essential by the

Government of India would be 'certified' under an elaborate system of procedure and carried in the Council of State, whether the Legislative Assembly objected or not. Surely such a cumbrous device is unnecessary. The suggestion for referring to the Secretary of State cases of conflict between the Legislative and the Executive (*ante*, p. 65) is infinitely simpler and more workable. The creation of the Council of State seems to be superfluous.

Detailed criticism of the fantastic 'diarchical' scheme of provincial government may be dispensed with. Sir J. P. Hewett points out that under it the position of the Governor would be intolerable. His government would be exposed to perpetual intrigue and deprived of all effective power.

**Fiscal autonomy.** The strongly expressed desire of Indian politicians for fiscal liberty has been briefly alluded to. The aspirations of 'educated Indians' on the subject are fairly summarized in paragraphs 341 and 342 of the Report. The demand is for a protective tariff, and for the concession of India's right to decide the matter for herself, whether her views be deemed economically sound or not. The authors of the Report refrain from making any recommendation on the matter because they understand that the fiscal relations of the British Empire will be considered after the war by a conference at which India will be represented. If the English nation deliberately makes up its mind to grant to India the utmost practicable measure of 'self-government', or 'self-determination', to use a still more fashionable phrase, it is not easy to see how fiscal autonomy can be refused.

**Economy *v.* progress.** Indian politicians almost without exception call for financial retrenchment, especially by reducing the military budget and the larger salaries drawn by high officials. Their lack of experience in government on a great scale leads them commonly both to underrate the military necessities of the country and to exaggerate the financial results of the savings so insistently demanded. The defence of the country would be ill provided for if it were at the mercy of the loudest talkers on the subject of finance. The current view among the 'educated Indian' class is clearly voiced by Mr. M. K. Gandhi, who is reported to have said (*Englishman*, Calcutta, July 20, 1918):

'The watchword of our reform councils will have to be, not increase for the growing needs of a growing country, but a decrease of financial burdens which are sapping the foundation itself of a genuine growth. This fundamental fact is recognized.'

The speaker certainly interpreted correctly the ordinary sentiment of his class. The allusion to 'increase for the growing needs of a growing country' apparently is directed against the views of the Aga Khan, who, almost alone among Indian reformers, denounces boldly the appalling backwardness of India in education, sanitation, public health, scientific development, and, in fact, in almost everything, while he at the same time sees clearly that expenditure on an imperial scale is required to bring his country up to date. Such expenditure cannot be defrayed from relatively small economies. It can be met only by additional revenue, the raising of which His Highness openly advocates. I wish I could agree with him in thinking that 'elective assemblies' will be willing and able to raise by fresh taxation the immense sums required to enable India to take her place among well-equipped modern nations. The exact contrary I believe to be the truth. The general Indian sentiment is *not* in favour of progress at the cost of taxation. Stagnation is preferred, and the initiative of progressive measures comes from above. The necessity for liberal expenditure on the development of the resources of India is fully discussed in the Report of the Indian Industrial Commission, a bulky document which reached London in December, 1918. The subject, although intimately connected with constitutional reform and the Indian aspirations for fiscal autonomy, cannot be pursued further in this place.

**Cow-killing.** Innumerable other recommendations or suggestions more or less closely associated with the proposed constitutional changes have been made by the authors of the Report or the writers of books and pamphlets. It is impossible to notice and criticize them all. One only, the demand for the prohibition of cow-killing and the sale of beef, requires mention, because that measure is passionately desired by practically all Hindus, who constitute the great majority of the population. If India could and should be governed under the conditions of ordinary democracy, which vest supreme power in the majority, it is unquestionable that the prohibition in question would be promulgated at the earliest possible opportunity. It is equally beyond question that such an enactment would be violently and fiercely resisted by the powerful Muslim minority of more than sixty-six millions.

It would also be opposed strenuously, although probably without violence, by the British army, the Christians in civil life, and several other important communities. Notwithstanding those certainties, Mr. Vyasa Rao ventures to declare it to be 'imperative that the slaughter of cows should be absolutely prohibited'. That cannot be done. The measure demanded so categorically would set all India in a blaze from one end to the other. It is useless to argue about the matter, or to invent more or less plausible economic arguments in support of the passionate Hindu sentiment. The question is, and for many centuries has been, governed by passion alone on both sides and reasoning is impotent. I have studied closely the history of the Hindu veneration of the cow from remote Vedic times, when beef used to be eaten on various special occasions, until the present day, when that diet is regarded with horror, and I could say much on the subject. But the less said the better. Almost any observation is apt to rouse a storm of angry controversy. The one thing beyond all doubt is that the boon which Hindus would value above any conceivable reform in political institutions cannot be granted.

The case is a striking illustration of the frequent incompatibility between Hindu traditional ideas and the conditions of modern life. It also illustrates better than anything else can do the imperious necessity for a strong, impartial government, in a position above all sections and able to protect the liberty of minorities. Home Rule in the sense of government by a pure majority, which in India would mean pure Hindu Rule, cannot be.

# CHAPTER 8

## CONSTRUCTIVE SUGGESTIONS

**Constructive suggestions necessary.** Merely destructive or analytical criticism of erroneous propositions or rash innovations is futile unless accompanied and supplemented by constructive suggestions of a practicable character. The Report is not the only possible solution of the problem of Indian constitutional reform. Everybody being agreed that changes in the direction of self-government within certain limits must be brought into operation, it is the bounden duty of all true friends of India to give what help may be in their power to the high authorities vested with the responsibility of decision. Such suggestions as are offered in this chapter are submitted for consideration with all deference and without dogmatism. If the language anywhere should seem dogmatic, the appearance is due only to a desire for concise expression. Small room exists for originality. Most of the conceivable proposals have been advocated by one person or another, and the writer of this essay has little of his own to add.

**Reserved powers.** Many limitations and guiding principles, as explained at considerable length in Chapter 7, must be constantly borne in mind by all would-be reformers. In addition to those observations it should be remembered that the Government of India must retain in its own hands, for use on special occasions, powers frankly described as 'autocracy' in the Report. That document reserves to the Government of India at least eight 'autocratic' powers, namely, (1) to repress anarchy; (2) to deal impartially with religious hostilities; (3) to protect the ryot; (4) to help the 'depressed classes', while giving them needful protection; (5) to defend sectional interests, especially the immense personal and material interests of the British and Anglo-Indian or Eurasian communities; (6) to give all proper support and protection to the members of the Services; (7) to defend India by sea and land; and (8) to exercise a general overriding power over all legislation.

I am not disposed to quarrel with any of those reservations, although it may be permissible to doubt if the Government of India will be in a position to fulfil all the promises thus implied.

**Limitations.** The limitations on complete self-government are, as already observed, imposed by inevitable conditions and are, in one sense of the term, independent of the form given to the administration, whether that of all India or that of a province. Proof has been adduced that anything like 'responsible government' in the English parliamentary sense is unthinkable within any period that can be now foreseen.

The Government of India, that is to say, the Governor-General in Council, as recognized by statute, is subordinate in its corporate character to Parliament through the Secretary of State.

**Governor-General and Viceroy.** The head of the government combines two distinct functions in his person. As Governor-General in Council, and in certain cases as Governor-General acting independently of his Council, he is subject to the control of the Secretary of State, and is sometimes even described as the agent of that high officer. As Viceroy he is the personal representative and Vicegerent of his Sovereign Lord, His Imperial Majesty the King-Emperor. The title of Viceroy, which is unknown to the statute book, was used for the first time in Queen Victoria's proclamation of 1858. It has now come into popular use as the ordinary designation of the head of the government, and the legal title of Governor-General or Governor-General in Council is rarely heard. But that change of practice does not affect the fact that the head of the government is both Governor-General and Viceroy. He has distinct duties to perform in each capacity, and the distinction, which is not merely technical, requires to be emphasized in the revised constitution. It is essential to remember that even after the assumption of the direct government of India by the Crown in 1858, material changes in the relations of the Sovereign with the princes and peoples of India were introduced by the Royal Titles Act of 1876 and subsequent events culminating in the solemn ceremonial at Delhi in December, 1911. Those constitutional changes, which are ignored in the Report, should be regarded as forming an essential element in the reformed constitution. It is also fitting and of practical importance that the distinction between the functions of the Governor-General and those of the Viceroy should receive formal and public recognition.

**British India and the States.** India consists of British India and of a multitude of Native or Protected States, enjoying autonomy in a greater or less degree. The States occupy about two-fifths of the total area. Their relations with the Government of India are determined by various instruments, which take the form of treaties in the more important cases. Those relations have arisen out of a long series of historical events, and, as a rule, cannot be altered without the express consent of the parties concerned. The large States, like the Nizam's Dominions, Mysore, Kashmir, and certain others, enjoy almost complete autonomy in the management of their internal affairs. The Government of India is bound ordinarily to abstain from interference in such affairs, while the rulers of the States, on their part, take no share in the administration of British India.

But the war has brought some of the princes into direct communication and working co-operation with the highest imperial authorities in London, so that those princes who have been admitted to the innermost councils of the British Empire are necessarily in a position to influence the policy of the Indian Empire. Indeed, certain princes have been consulted by the Government of India recently on matters concerning British India.

The rulers of the States all willingly acknowledge the duty of paying homage to the King-Emperor, and recognize that His Imperial Majesty is represented in India by his vicegerent the Viceroy. They also have constant communications more of a business character with the Governor-General in Council, and so indirectly with the Secretary of State and Parliament. The Protected States, although legally distinct from British India, are associated intimately with that area in a thousand ways. For instance, the currency, railway, telegraph, post office, and other departments of British India cannot be disentangled from the same departments operating in the States. The complications thus indicated have a considerable bearing upon any scheme of constitutional reform for British India. Although no such scheme can be applied directly to the States, nevertheless it concerns them in its operation. The Report devotes Chapter X (paragraphs 296–312) to discussion of the relations of the Government of India with the States.

**Evolution.** When we consider the extreme complexity of the problem of constitutional reform due to the fact that all the conditions indicated and others not mentioned have to be kept in mind, it will seem obvious to most people that the delicate mechanism of the existing Indian constitution should be exposed to the least possible disturbance, and that reform should take the shape of evolution rather than of revolution.

**Provincial reforms.** As regards the provinces, general

agreement exists that the Governor should be given an executive council, if he has not one already; that, provided fit persons are available, at least one member of each executive council should, as a matter of practice, be of Indian birth; and that the existing legislative councils should be enlarged and made more representative. The definite separation of provincial from imperial finance is similarly approved, and a relaxation of the control exercised by the Governments of India over the provincial governments is conceded. Those propositions appear to be unobjectionable.

**Franchise.** It may be taken as settled that the appointment of councillors by means of election will be largely extended, and that the franchise will be considerably widened. It is not likely that it will be extended to women. Discussion of details must be reserved pending the receipt of supplementary reports from the commissions now (December, 1918) operating in India. One franchise question only, concerning which the recommendation of the Report is open to objection, will be noticed presently.

**The writer's suggestions.** Subject to the foregoing general observations, I feel justified in submitting certain substantive suggestions, mostly selected from those made by other people, which commend themselves to my judgement. They are offered in the hope that they may aid in the formation of sound public and parliamentary opinion, which is the necessary preparation for the drafting of a good India Bill. A few suggestions recorded in earlier chapters need not be repeated here.

**Scrutiny of the Report.** In October, 1918, when the Cabinet declined to submit the Report in its present state of incompleteness pending the receipt of the supplements to the scrutiny of a joint committee of both Houses of Parliament, Lord Curzon of Kedleston announced that such a committee would not be called into existence until *after* the second reading of the Government's India Bill. At the same time he held out hopes that means might be found to secure a preliminary hearing of objections. The Report will not be considered by the Cabinet until it is completed by the supplementary reports expected to reach England in the spring.

It seems right that facilities should be granted for a close scrutiny of the principles and proposals of the completed Report *before* it is adopted as the basis of a Government Bill, or, at any rate, *before* the second reading. The precise nature of the machinery approved for the needed scrutiny is of minor importance. If the scrutiny is deferred until *after* the second reading of the Bill, the Government and Parliament will then be committed to all the main provisions of the measure, and further discussion will be confined to details. While all parties are agreed on the necessity of reform in the direction of self-government and the extended employment of Indians in the public service, excessive haste is to be deprecated, and it is desirable that the Bill in its main outlines should be non-contentious as far as possible.

**Periodical commissions.** If, as seems probable, the suggestion of the Report (paragraph 295) be adopted, and a Sessional Committee be appointed, whether of the House of Commons only, or preferably of both Houses, it would seem wise to drop the proposals for sending out frequent committees or commissions 'to deal with the political progress of India' (paragraphs 288, 294). Such commissions would not only harass the Government of India beyond endurance, as already observed, but in all probability would hinder the 'political progress' of the country. That somewhat tender plant should be allowed to grow in peace, and suitable arrangements to meet changed conditions can be made when actually required. A binding undertaking to appoint a commission of inquiry at a definite time a few years hence tends to unsettle men's minds and to stimulate pernicious agitation.

**Burma.** The separation or 'divorce', as Mr. Curtis calls it, of Burma from the Indian Empire appears to be judicious in the interests of both India and Burma. It would be advantageous to India for many reasons, one being that the government of the Indian Empire is overloaded and has more work to do than it can manage efficiently. The withdrawal of Burma from the control of the Delhi government would give immense relief. Very few persons concerned in the administration of India proper possess any considerable knowledge of Burma or understand the peculiar conditions and needs of that vast territory. The Burmese Empire, as it used to be called, has little in common with India. The absence of caste in Burma is in itself a fundamental difference. The Burmese culture or form of civilization is more allied to the Chinese than to the Indian. The principal elements of the population are Mongolian, and the religion is Buddhism of the Ceylon type. The manners, customs, and temperament of the people are absolutely different from those of the Indian peoples. It would be extremely difficult to devise a scheme of constitutional reform on modern lines which should suit Burma even tolerably. The absolute exclusion of the Burmese territories from consideration would simplify materially the problems of reform, which are difficult enough when India alone is the subject of experiment.

The histories of India and Burma rarely touch. The British conquest of the Burmese Empire was effected in three instalments in the years 1826, 1852, and 1886. Prior to those dates the contact between India and Burma in historical times was of the slightest possible character, being almost confined to border raids and fights with Arakanese pirates. No historical sentiment would be violated by the proposed divorce.

Burma, potentially one of the richest countries in the world, unquestionably would gain by being freed from the rather step-motherly care of the Government of India.

It is notorious that Burmese affairs receive but a small share of attention from the overburdened officials at Delhi or Simla, and it is certain that a government in Burma, when released from Indian shackles, would be able to do far more for the country than the Governor can do now. Although the Aga Khan is opposed to the suggested separation, he does not offer any substantive reasons for maintaining the existing ill-matched union.

If separation be decided on in principle, all subsidiary difficulties about finance, military or naval requirements, and the public services can be overcome. No large change can be effected without a good deal of trouble, and elaborate demonstrations that the severance of the Burmese chain would result in a crop of temporary difficulties need not stand in the way of a highly advantageous reform.

The Province of Burma, the former Burmese Empire, is a huge charge as it stands, but it might be judicious to place the whole of the Malay peninsula, so far as it is subject to British control, under the same government. The Governor of Burma would then become a Governor-General, aided by a Governor or Lieutenant-Governor of the Malay peninsula, and other officers of similar rank in the Burmese provinces. As the country progressed, it is probable that before many years had elapsed the Governor-General of Burma would have four or five governors or lieutenant-governors under his control.

**Ceylon.** After the conquest of the Dutch settlements, the island of Ceylon, excepting the kingdom of Kandy, remained for a short time, from 1796 to 1798, a dependency of Madras. If Lord Wellesley could have had his way it would then have come permanently under the rule of the East India Company, but his plans were disallowed. In 1815 the whole island, including the dominions of the recently deposed king of Kandy, passed under the dominion of King George III, and since that date it has been a Crown

Colony, controlled by the Secretary of State for the Colonies. The Government of India has no concern with its affairs. The Aga Khan would like to include the colony in the Indian Empire, but very grave objections probably would be taken to that arrangement by the people concerned. Ceylon is closely connected with Burma by the bond of religion, and it is possible that it might be expedient to attach the island to the Governor-Generalship of Burma. Change, however, does not appear to be urgently required, and the question of transfer, if ever raised definitely, can wait for leisurely investigation.

**H.M. the King-Emperor.** The principle of utilizing to the fullest possible extent the genuine feelings of loyalty to H.M. the King-Emperor entertained by all classes of Indians probably will be acknowledged to be sound. It seems right that India should have her own flag, and that on all great occasions of ceremony both the flag of India and, if permitted, the Royal Standard should be flown. The latter when used, of course, should be given precedence over the Viceregal standard. Other symbolical arrangements in accordance with ancient Indian tradition could be made which should make plain to all beholders that the Viceroy was acting on such occasions as the personal representative of his Sovereign, and not merely as the head of the impersonal Government of India. For instance, the placing of an empty throne bearing the imperial crown behind and above the Viceregal chair of state would be intelligible to everybody and agreeable to custom.[1] Other similar expressions of the living authority of the absent Sovereign could be easily devised and worked out. Systematic arrangements should be made to bring home to pupils in schools and colleges the personality of the King-Emperor by portraits and other means. A simple, well-written account of the

[1] Such a symbolical presence of the Sovereign might be held to justify flying the Royal Standard.

lives of His Majesty and of the Queen might be prepared in the principal vernacular languages and circulated widely. If it is once admitted that it would be wise to make a serious effort in the direction indicated, ways and means will be easily found.

**Royal Viceroy.** The most important conceivable measure in furtherance of the idea would be the appointment of a prince of the blood royal as Viceroy. That proposal, warmly advocated by both His Highness the Aga Khan and Mr. Vyasa Rao, undoubtedly commends itself to Indian feeling, and its adoption would go a long way towards abating the natural dislike for foreign rule.

The appointment of a Royal Viceroy involves necessarily the corollary that the Viceroy should be relieved of most of the administrative work for British India which he now performs in his capacity of Governor-General in Council.

**Viceregal duties.** The Royal Viceroy should retain control of honours, dignities, pardons, and the department dealing with the Native or Protected States. A large part of his time would be occupied by personal intercourse with their rulers. If either a Council of State or an advisory Council of Princes, or both bodies, should be constituted, as suggested in the Report, the Viceroy would naturally preside. At present the Foreign Department of the Government of India always is retained by the Governor-General in his own hands, and is not made over to a member of council, as is each of the other principal departments. The Foreign Secretary, under the direction of the Governor-General, deals both with the Protected States and with really foreign affairs. The time seems to have come when the affairs of the Protected States should no longer be considered as those of foreign territory. The changes in the relations between the Crown and the Princes wrought by the Royal Titles Act and subsequent events have made the old-fashioned arrangements an anachronism and practically inconsistent with the altered conditions. The suggestion may be offered that a States Secretary should be appointed distinct from the Foreign Secretary. The results of the war promise to increase materially the foreign connexions of the Government of India, and to give abundant occupation for a separate Secretary or Minister. The retention by the Viceroy as such of the department of Foreign Affairs in the strict sense probably would be advisable. Two suggestions are tendered concerning the machinery by which the Royal Viceroy might be relieved of the ordinary administration of British India. The Aga Khan proposes that that class of business should be made over to a Prime Minister appointed by the Crown for the same term of office as the Viceroy, and assisted by other ministers selected by the Viceroy and Prime Minister. The Viceroy would continue to hold the statutory office of Governor-General, but would perform its functions through his deputy, the Prime Minister. Thus, so far as British India is concerned, his position would be nearly that of a constitutional monarch. If the Viceroy as such should retain personal control of the Protected States and also of foreign relations, he would have two ministers of his own, the States Secretary and the Secretary for Foreign Affairs. Probably it would be expedient that in his capacity as Viceroy the head of the Government should correspond with the Prime Minister of the United Kingdom, and not with the Secretary of State for India, copies of his dispatches being supplied to the India Office for information.

**A separate Governor-General.** The plan recommended by Mr. Vyasa Rao is more ambitious and involves a wider divergence from usage. He would recommend the appointment of a separate Governor-General, taking precedence after the Viceroy. Either arrangement seems to be feasible, but it is difficult for any person who has not shared in the work of the highest authorities to form a valuable opinion concerning the exact way in which the necessary change should be carried out. If the principles be conceded that the distinction between the two offices of Viceroy and Governor-General should be clearly recognized and that the viceregal appointment should be held ordinarily by a prince of the blood royal, relieved from the general administration of British India, the consequential arrangements can be put into workable form without much difficulty by persons equipped with the needful experience.

Ministers of either the Viceroy or the Governor-General, corresponding in function to the members of the existing Imperial Executive Council, should not be eligible for promotion or transfer to another appointment. The present system of frequently selecting the rulers of provinces from members of the Government of India is open to grave objections.

The viceregal officers who have been referred to as the States Secretary and the Secretary for Foreign Affairs would be actually ministers, whatever their official designation might be.

The proposed reform in any shape, like all reforms worth having, would cost money, but it would be well spent. The Government of India as at present constituted is admittedly overworked and undermanned. It retains far too many traces of the archaic and obsolete machinery dating from the times of the East India Company.

**Importance of the reform.** So far as I am able to judge of matters lying outside the range of my personal experience, the reforms sketched above, whatever shape they might ultimately assume, would be of the highest possible significance and would do much to make all India feel that it had won its rightful place 'within the Empire' under the direct rule of a venerated Sovereign.

An unusually sympathetic and well-informed observer, the Rev. W. E. S. Holland, has justly said that 'the heart of India is passionately set upon self-expression as a nation'. That legitimate sentiment, which finds almost insuperable difficulties in uttering itself through the foreign mechanism of parliamentarism, on which the Report lays undue stress, would obtain adequate utterance by means of the 'great constitutional device, pregnant with enduring possibilities of good' outlined in the foregoing pages.

**Sentiment.** In Ireland and India, countries which have much in common, notwithstanding the enormous difference of scale, the magic power of sentiment has been too often ignored by unimaginative statesmen, entangled in the wheels of parliamentary machinery and absorbed in the struggle for materialistic progress.

**The British community.** The immense British interests, both personal and material, in India require more sympathetic consideration than they have received in the Report. Modern India is the creation mainly of British energy and capital, working alike in the official and economic domains. The important British community, including both pure Europeans and the Anglo-Indians or Eurasians of mixed descent, rightly demands adequate recognition of itself as constituting one of the principal elements in the population, and carrying weight in the national councils far greater than that indicated by its mere numbers. Such recognition, somewhat grudgingly and imperfectly conceded in paragraph 232 of the Report, is qualified by observations which seem to be hardly consistent with the concession. The authors, when discussing the representation of minorities, say that for

'the representation of other minorities we should prefer nomination. Even in the case of the general European community, whose material interests in the country are out of all proportion to their numerical strength and on whose behalf it may be argued that no departure from principle is involved, inasmuch as unlike all other communities named they are not an integral part of the population of India, we prefer to rely upon nomination. Special electorates will no doubt be required for the representation of the planting and mining interests, for the chambers of commerce, and possibly also for the universities; but we desire that the number of such electorates should be as restricted as possible, and that minority interests should, where necessary, be represented not by class or interest electorates but by nomination.'

That recommendation is vigorously and indignantly opposed by the parties most concerned, who have expressed their objections on more than one occasion, supporting them by arguments which may be fairly called conclusive. Surely it is unreasonable that the one section of the population thoroughly acquainted with representative government in theory and practice should be debarred from the privilege of electing their representatives. Parliament is not likely to reject the just claim of the British community. The assertion that that community does not form 'an integral part of the population of India' is inexact and should not have been made.

**Diarchy.** It is to be hoped that the almost universally condemned scheme for dividing each provincial government into two sections, which is the most controversial proposal in the Report, will be dropped quietly. Discussion has shown that the scheme, conveniently labelled 'diarchy', could not be worked without intolerable friction (unless Bombay be an exception, as is claimed). The elimination of that unfortunate proposal, dictated by the over-logical pursuit of a doctrinaire theory, would materially facilitate the passage of the India Bill.

**Local administration.** As regards local administration, the proposition that local bodies should be allowed reasonable liberty cannot be formally disputed. But in India, where frightful epidemics are of constant occurrence, the obligation to preserve a decent sanitary standard in towns at any rate is an imperial one. Burdwan, an important town in Bengal, with about 35,000 inhabitants, has lately exhibited such a deplorable example of municipal inefficiency and pecuniary corruption that the town council has been suspended. Strict control is indispensable, and it appears necessary that local administration in each province should be efficiently controlled by a special minister or similar official at head-quarters. His designation is immaterial. Whenever a competent person of Indian birth can be found let him be appointed by all means, but no racial qualification is permissible by law, and regard for the public health imperatively requires efficiency in control.

**Panchāyats.** It may possibly be feasible to revive village autonomy to a certain extent on the lines suggested by Mr. Vyasa Rao. The provincial governments presumably would be willing to try the experiment, if it offers a reasonable prospect of success. The difficulty may arise among the villagers themselves. Unpaid service is not popular in India, and it is not unlikely that suitors may prefer recourse to the courts they know and may be unwilling to dispense with the aid of lawyers, on which they are accustomed to rely.

**Indian Civil Service.** The most thorny subject, perhaps, is that of the Services, and especially that of the Civil Service of India, now called the Indian Civil Service. The discussion of Section 87 of the Charter Act of 1833 (*ante*, p. 71) may be referred to with advantage, and the reader is asked to remember that the law absolutely forbids racial qualification or disqualification under any pretext. That fundamental principle, although often forgotten or ignored, must govern all lawful proposals.

The general administration of the country at the present time being now, as it has been since the eighteenth century, mostly in the hands of the members of the Indian Civil Service, an able, highly trained body of experts with a most honourable record, it is admitted by all writers that it would be impossible to carry on the administration and initiate a great scheme of constitutional reform without the aid of that body. The time when such a *corps d'élite* can be summarily discarded obviously has not come yet and, so far as can be foreseen, is not likely to come for many years, if the life of the Service can be preserved as long. Competent critics perceive clearly, as they could not fail to perceive, that it will be very difficult to keep the Civil Service in existence under the conditions foreshadowed by the Report. The attractions of the Service undoubtedly must be seriously diminished. Even now such moderate attractions as exist have little charm, and first-class men believe that they can do better in other professions. While India urgently wants the Civil Service for an indefinite time, it is quite possible that the Service may die of inanition, simply from lack of competent British recruits. The difficulties of recruitment have been enhanced immensely by the war, and there is grave reason to fear that the quality of the men engaged has deteriorated.

**Judicial functions.** A reform or change insistently pressed for many years past is the separation of judicial from executive functions. At present many officers exercise both, in accordance with immemorial Indian tradition. The change, if carried out to the extreme logical result, would completely transform the Indian Civil Service. The existing arrangements provide congenial careers for men of diverse tastes. All the young officers begin their service as Assistant Magistrates and Collectors, performing a great variety of duties, including judicial business in their capacity of magistrates and also in most provinces as revenue and rent courts. Excluding certain fortunate persons who become Secretaries to Government or attain other eminent positions outside of the regular line, the members of the Service, after gaining a few years of general experience, usually are called upon to decide between a judicial and an administrative career. The judicial type of man rises in the ordinary course to the rank of District and Sessions judge, whose office has not any equivalent in England. If exceptionally lucky he may become a High Court Judge. His fellow civilian of the more active executive type often does not go beyond the rank of District officer, whose duties resemble in many respects those of a French *préfet* ; but certain more successful men attain to high appointments of various kinds, some becoming rulers of great provinces, and others ministers in the Government of India. Most of the appointments referred to were formerly reserved by law (Act of 1861) for members of the Service, but since 1870 the exclusive privileges of the Service have been gradually reduced, and many outsiders have been given appointments which used to be reserved for its members.

Even still, notwithstanding numerous changes, the greater part of the higher administrative and executive posts is held by the Indian Civil Service. 'Civilians', as the members are commonly called in India, also fill many of the High Court and District Judgeships. For a long time past a strong tendency has been manifested in favour of increasing the Indian element in the judicial branch of the Service. Many reformers urge that all judicial appointments should be made from the legal profession as in England. If that recommendation be adopted and judgeships cease to be open to the Indian Civil Service, the attractions of the Service will be very materially diminished, and the judicial type of man will no longer compete for an appointment.

If the separation of judicial and executive functions be completed in every direction, it will be necessary to appoint a large number of separate magistrates, and a multitude of other officials in the 'temporarily settled' provinces, to try rent and 'revenue' cases, which are very different from ordinary civil court causes, and require special knowledge of rural economy, as possessed by numerous members of the Indian Civil Service and rarely found elsewhere. Incidentally, it may be observed that the change will involve large extra expense. The District officer, the history of whose office as the local representative of government goes back to remote antiquity, would thus cease to be a magistrate or to hear rent and 'revenue' cases. His duties would be confined to action as the executive agent of the government for collecting land revenue and taxes, and for the general supervision of certain branches of the administration within his district. The functions of his assistants in all grades would be similarly circumscribed. Such specialization of function, which is the normal practice in Europe, would involve a complete departure from immemorial Indian tradition, and certainly would be disliked intensely by the great mass of the people. But it is not unlikely that the 'educated classes' will succeed in forcing the change, to which they attach much importance. If so, the post of District officer, which many members of the Service consider the most interesting that a man can hold, will no longer possess any charm. If again, as the Aga Khan suggests, the office of Commissioner be abolished in the provinces where it exists; and if further, as Mr. Vyasa Rao proposes, members of the Indian Civil Service are to be debarred from becoming rulers of provinces, it is not easy to see why any young Englishman of ability and ambition should enter the Service.

**Dilemma.** Thus we are brought face to face with the dilemma that while India badly wants the Service with its high standard of ability, its expert training, and its noble tradition, in order to carry on the administration and start the 'reforms', those very reforms threaten to dry up the sources from which the Service is supplied. No solution of the impasse is visible, and it seems desirable that the question of keeping the Indian Civil Service in effective existence or allowing it to expire should be faced squarely and thoroughly investigated by a small authoritative committee in England. The cases of the Educational, Police, and Medical services also require special discussion by a similar method for various reasons in each case. The purely technical branches of the public service, such as Telegraph, Forests, Public Works, &c., present easier problems, which can be solved by strict attention to the principles of fair play without racial discrimination in any form, of selection of the best men, and of offering such material advantages as will attract really good officers, whatever may be their colour. India cannot afford to be served badly by cheap, half-trained departmental officials.

**Haileybury redivivum.** One measure only, so far as I can see at the moment, promises well for the future of the Services in India, if the Government can be persuaded to adopt it, which does not seem likely. That is the plan so eloquently advocated by Mr. Archer (*ante*, p. 70) for the establishment of a great training college, which might be described as a revived, enlarged, and modernized Haileybury. In such a college the probationers for the Indian Civil Service, if any, and all the youths destined for other branches of the public service should receive their training. At the Universities India is regarded as a subject devoid of general interest, and the young men destined for the Indian services who pursue their special studies at a University never learn to feel that India should have the first place in their thoughts. The whole atmosphere of their surroundings discourages such a sentiment, and in fact prevents its birth. The students at the proposed college, on the contrary, would feel that they were dedicated to India, and that they were working 'in a place where India should always be present, predominant, enthroned'. I have shared Mr. Archer's opinion independently for a great many years, and am glad to see that it has the support of Lord Sydenham of

Combe. To my thinking the reform would be so valuable that even if it cost a million sterling it would be worth the money. But I know that the idea has powerful opponents, and so I must leave the matter, with some faint hope that it may at one time or another receive the favourable consideration hitherto denied.

**Summary.** After so much discussion and criticism it is advisable to sum up the results, even at the cost of a certain amount of repetition.

The necessity for extensive change in the old-fashioned method of governing India is admitted.

Reform should follow the lines of evolution, not of revolution.

Burma should be separated from the Indian Empire.

The limits of practicable change are narrowly fixed by barriers of hard facts. The caste institution is, perhaps, the most intractable of such barriers. The facts cannot be altered by words, even those of an Act of Parliament. If a candid statement of realities be found disagreeable, that is the fault of the realities, not of the pen which records them faithfully.

The term 'self-government' has two meanings. Regarded as meaning the release of an Indian administration, Imperial or Provincial, however it may be constituted internally, from excessive supervision, it is readily attainable by the agency of legislation or executive order. Regarded as meaning the direction of policy and administration by born Indians, it is subject to many limitations, and is difficult of attainment, which is conditioned by the internal constitution of the administration and by the personnel of the Services.

The 'goal of Responsible Government' is a distant vision, which, in my opinion, should be left alone for the present. If that course should be followed much embarrassment would be avoided. The contradictions and makeshift devices which disfigure the Report are due almost entirely to the premature chase after 'responsible government'. It is possible that in Bombay, the most advanced province as a whole, something in the nature of 'responsible government' may be feasible at a date much earlier than in other provinces. 'Self-government' and the increased employment of Indians in the public service are quite enough to occupy all the time of the present-day reformer.

Section 87 of the Charter Act of 1833 *must* be obeyed strictly and impartially. Special care should be taken to avoid the creation of new and illegal racial disqualifications as against Europeans, using that term in a wide sense.

The control exercised by the Secretary of State and the India Office over the Government of India should be materially relaxed, and that Government should be allowed far more liberty than it enjoys now. In this connexion the burning question relates to fiscal policy, because India demands power to impose a tariff, as an act of 'self-determination', and a matter of right.

The Government of India should be 'responsible' in the sense of being sensitive to Indian public opinion, and of being so constituted as to allow that opinion full expression.

Nevertheless, the conditions are such that the Government of India must retain extensive 'autocratic' powers.

The internal constitution of that Government need not necessarily follow precisely the lines of the Report, which at this date (December, 1918) is not binding in any way on the Cabinet, Parliament, or the nation.

The fact that 'the heart of India is passionately set on self-expression as a nation' should be frankly recognized. Although, for reasons expounded in this book, anything like complete national unity is unattainable, the sentiment which reaches out towards that goal is legitimate, ennobling, and worthy of encouragement 'within the Empire'. It has been partially gratified by various recent executive measures, which have given Indian statesmen their full share in shaping the destinies of the British Empire. India should have her national flag.

The authority of the Crown, that is to say, of a living, personal Sovereign, is the most potent unifying force operating in India. The distinction between the Viceroy and the Governor-General should be legally acknowledged and publicly manifested. The Viceroy should be ordinarily a Prince of the blood royal, and be relieved of the greater part of the administration of British India, as vested by law in the Governor-General in Council. If the Prince should also be Governor-General, he would perform his duties as such through a Prime Minister or deputy Governor-General. If another person be appointed Governor-General, he would rank below the Viceroy. Either scheme seems to be feasible. Suitable means should be devised and used to emphasize the reality of the Royal authority, especially as regards the Protected States. Their affairs should no longer be managod by the Foreign Secretary, but should be conducted by a separate States Secretary. The procedure should be in accordance with the changes which have taken place since 1858.

The Imperial Legislative Council should be expanded into a much larger Legislative Assembly, mainly elected. The official majority should be abandoned, the number of officials attending the meetings and entitled to speak but not to vote being regulated by practical requirements. Only non-official members should vote. Differences on important questions between the executive government and the Assembly should be referred either to the Secretary of State or to a Board of Arbitration in England. The Council of State or Senate as proposed in the Report is not wanted.

If ornamental bodies, such as an Indian Privy Council or an Advisory Council of Princes, be created, they cannot do either much good or much harm.

The Governor of each important province should have an Executive Council, and his Legislative Council should be enlarged on the same lines as the Imperial Council. Differences between the Executive and the Legislature should be referred to the Government of India for final decision.

The franchise should be extended, but details must remain open for the present. Purely territorial constituencies are impracticable. Territoriality must be modified by both 'communal' and 'institutional' representation. In some cases it may even be necessary to grant communal representation to *majorities* as well as to minorities.

The concession of greater liberty to local bodies must be guarded by strict supervision in the interests of the public health and for other reasons.

The most difficult problem is that of the Services, and especially of the Indian Civil Service. That *corps d'élite* is at present indispensable, while at the same time its very existence is threatened. The consideration of the dilemma should be made over to a small authoritative committee sitting in London. The method of selecting probationers for the Soudanese service is an improvement on the purely examination test by which admission is gained to the Indian Civil Service. Either the same committee or similar bodies should examine the cases of the Police, Educational, and Indian Medical Services.

All probationers and candidates for the Indian appointments made in England should be trained together at a special college, preferably situated at Oxford.

Such a foundation need not clash with the School of Oriental Studies in London. There is room for both.

# INDEX